Nudges
from
HEAVEN

Nudges

from

HEAVEN

TAMMY ROY

Printed in Canada

ISBN: 978-1-4866-2080-7
eBook ISBN: 978-1-4866-2081-4

Word Alive Press
119 De Baets Street Winnipeg, MB R2J 3R9
www.wordalivepress.ca

Cataloguing in Publication information can be obtained from Library and Archives Canada.

DEDICATION

This book is dedicated to the heartbeat of my world—my husband and children!

Greg: Can you believe it? So much has transpired since we both said those two words, "I do!" December 21, 1991, was the day that completely changed my world. In front of family, friends, and God, we committed our lives to each other.

Those personalized, handwritten vows have been put to the test on more than one occasion. I thank God every day for you; you could've run, but instead, you chose to show me what true love looks like. You have loved me through crazy and calm, through sickness and health, through talking and silence (though, let's be honest, when have I ever been silent?). Through laughter and tears, and now through the writing of my first book, you've been there. Thank you for encouraging me to dream big and pursue God's purposes. You will always be my forever. I love you!

To my three amazing kids, Tyler, Jordan, and Brooke, you are the "cheese to my chippies," so you know that's a whole lotta love!

Tyler: Who knew that when you boarded the plane to Australia eight years ago, God was leading you into your destiny? It has been the most difficult, yet rewarding, season of releasing you into God's call for your life.

Since the day I found out that our family was growing from two to three, I dedicated you to the Lord. Never could I have imagined that I would be stuck in a pandemic lockdown, unable to be with you on your most important day. Witnessing your wedding from across the globe via live stream, as you and your beautiful bride, Rachel, said, "I do," brought tears of joy to this aching mama's heart. I love how God orchestrated the intersecting of your two worlds, and I'm so excited to watch His plan unfold in your lives. I love you both and I'm incredibly proud to be your mother!

Jordan: You are my miracle man, an answer to my prayers. I remember the night I thought I was losing you; it looked as though I was heading down the dark, despairing road of losing another child through miscarriage, and I begged God to spare your life. I didn't get off my knees until I heard an answer. God heard my cries and stilled the raging sea of my anxious heart.

His plans for you are good, Jord. It seems those early years have gone by in a blink, but they've left in their wake memories to fill this mama's love tank. Like you said in your best man's speech to your brother at his wedding: "I thought those days would never end." Thank you for filling my heart with precious memories. I love you!

Brooke: What a journey you have been on! You have found the treasure worth more than this world can offer. Your heart is set on pilgrimage and you haven't looked back. I am constantly in awe of the woman you have become. The way you extend love and grace toward others amazes me. You have learned what it means to forgive, and it has come at a cost. You are an extravagant giver who loves to bless others, and I couldn't be prouder to be your mama. From the moment I first held you in my arms, I recognized the miracle you were, and I have seen the faithfulness of God played out in your life. You have been called and marked with purpose and destiny. I love you!

And to Jesus: Thank You for giving me the words to write; without you, there would be no stories to share.

ACKNOWLEDGMENTS

Thank you to the following wonderful people in my life:

Eryn Wilder, for cheering me on from heaven. You were there at the start of this crazy book journey and witnessed a complete stranger tell me, "God told you to write a book. Now write!" You encouraged me, prayed for me, and believed in me. I know you're now celebrating with me.

Brian and Leah Robertson... Words don't do justice to who you are and all you've invested and sown into my life. I love you and your family fiercely! You are the real deal. Thank you for your love and encouragement when I felt like giving up. You are amazing pastors and I'm so thankful you're part of my tribe. Your listening ears and constructive feedback were instrumental throughout the entire process. I'm so grateful for your love, friendship, and dinners.

Robin Roy... My one and only brother-in-law. Thank you for your generous provision of the laptop. It prevented hours of frustration and enabled me to tap away to my heart's content and see this baby through.

John Mercer... A true friend through and through! Thank you for believing in, supporting, and encouraging me through this daunting process. Your feedback was valuable, but your jokes, priceless!

Dad and (Mom)... Last, but certainly not least! What would my book be without acknowledging my parents, who gave me a passion for Jesus? Dad, I am grateful for the endless stories you told while I was growing up. You are the ultimate storyteller and your support for this book has meant the world to me. I know Mom is in heaven dancing a happy dance as she celebrates this milestone. Thank you, from your half-pint.

FOREWORD

One of the most inspiring things about Tammy Roy is that she rarely misses the "God story" in the regular (and not-so-regular) occurrences of life. Spend ten minutes with her and you're bound to hear of how she saw God moving in her day.

She's an ordinary woman from a small town on Vancouver Island, B.C. An ordinary woman who has chosen to see life through the lens of wonder. An ordinary woman who sees around her the hand and the voice of an extraordinary God.

There is much in Tammy's past and present that could take her down a vastly different path. Experiences that could have led to cynicism, discouragement, fatalism, depression, and anger. What we see in her, though, is a child-like faith and assurance in the Lord's declaration in Jeremiah 29:11: "*For I know the plans I have for you," declares the Lord, 'plans to prosper you and not to harm you, plans to give you hope and a future.'*"

Her confidence is contagious. On many occasions, it has encouraged us to recalibrate our perspective. It has given her children a boldness and surety in stepping out in their own faith journeys. It has inspired others to see the possible in their impossibilities.

Tammy has recorded here a glimpse into her story. A story of family, work, health issues, chance encounters, and life decisions, punctuated with the voice of a good, good Father. In so many ways, these stories are like any of ours. They are the stuff of ordinary life. But in so many other ways, these stories attempt to draw us into the possibility that God is speaking in all these ordinary events. Tammy's accounts encourage us to believe that we can all hear that voice, that each one of us can experience the nudges of heaven.

Read and be encouraged.

Brian and Leah Robertson, Pastors, Christian Fellowship Centre, Qualicum Beach, B.C.

PREFACE

There is something in each of us that longs to be the hero in our own story. We are all living in the middle of a story—our story. There are empty pages yet to be written and no one can complete them for you; only *you* have been given the pen. There have been times you may have put the pen down, or even times you've thrown the pen against the wall in frustration. Perhaps you've looked back at your past and have wanted a rewrite, a do-over. This is a reminder that you still have ink in your pen. Each morning you wake up is a wonderful opportunity to change the ongoing theme of your story until your ink runs out.

My ink resembled more of an Etch A Sketch when my story began...

As far back as I can remember, I have recognized God's presence in my life, even as a little girl—and I mean *little*. There's nothing quite like having your first adventure with heaven while you're still in the crib. That first memory set the foundation of truth that I was not a mistake, but was planned and perfectly designed by God, who loves me and will never leave me! I have countless memories of incredible moments when heaven touched down and intertwined with the adventures of a little girl affectionately called "half-pint" by her daddy.

Biblical principles were established in my childhood as part of my "ordinary." However, my childhood was anything but ordinary; had I kept a journal, I could've written several books before I was ten. The moments when heaven stepped in and intervened are etched in my memory as though they happened yesterday. This book is filled with these moments.

I'm thankful for all of the incredible encounters, conversations, dreams, visions, and prayer times that, when all pieced together, have made the most beautiful mosaic called "My Story." I pray that the words of this book will impact your spirit as you come face to face with The One who loves you and calls you by name. He wants you to know your true identity. He will place your feet upon the unshakeable foundation of truth that you are deeply loved and not a mistake. You are fiercely loved and not abandoned. You are forever loved and His plans for you are always good!

> *For you created my inmost being;*
> *you knit me together in my mother's womb.*
> *I praise you because I am fearfully and wonderfully made;*
> *your works are wonderful,*
> *I know that full well.*
> *My frame was not hidden from you*
> *when I was made in the secret place,*
> *when I was woven together in the depths of the earth.*

Your eyes saw my unformed body;
all the days ordained for me were written in your book
before one of them came to be. (Psalm 139:13–16)

This is my story…

JUST AN
Ordinary
ISLAND GIRL

There's something so beautifully innocent about a little girl sitting on a swing, kicking her legs back and forth, pumping with all of her might as she swings higher and higher, absorbed in the moment of feeling so alive, with swirling thoughts of the future soaring above the white, puffy, animal-shaped clouds.

Many young girls have done this, imagining who they would become one day.

For me, I was one of "Charlie's Angels." In my mind, what girl wouldn't have wanted to be one of the three most gorgeous female private detectives on television? I used to peddle my tricycle around our gravel roundabout driveway in pursuit of the "bad guys," and before each turn, I said, "Blinking, blinking, blinking," as the indicator lights on my imaginary Ford Mustang caught up with the suspects in record time. I turned my head back to "swoosh" my non-existent long hair, pointed my imaginary gun, and became the hero once again.

Shortly after I outgrew my tricycle, my "career choice" changed. I wanted to be a preacher like my dad. He had an incredible gift of storytelling, which he incorporated into his sermons. Often, I was literally on the edge of my seat, whether at home or at church, as I listened to him bring the Bible to life. He could connect everyday modern life to stories in the Bible, and I wanted to follow in his footsteps.

One afternoon, when I was seven years old, I found some pieces of wood in our little woodshed beside our house and built myself a pulpit. This wasn't your typical, Sunday-morning church pulpit; no, this had pizazz! I had taken felt pens and coloured the entire structure with purple flowers. Nothing says "pulpit" quite like an artistic arrangement of a garden display.

I had quite the imagination. I regularly set up the pulpit in our rumpus room and preached to my imaginary congregation. That ended abruptly, however, after I realized my brother had been spying on me and listening to my fiery sermons. Yet I can honestly, to this day, say that I felt the presence of God during my downstairs church services. Maybe this is what every PK (Preacher's Kid) ends up doing, wishing to follow in their father's or mother's footsteps.

Although preaching to my imaginary congregation stopped, the passion for it didn't change. For as long as I can remember, I had always wanted to share my faith with others. It's something that's etched into the very fibre of my being. Introducing people to Jesus makes me tick; it makes me happy; it makes me whole.

I felt the nudges of heaven to tell others about God from a young age. Those first nudges started when I was five years old. I remember sitting in our family car, waiting for my mom after she had said her familiar, "Wait here, I'll be right back" as she popped into the department store. As I was patiently waiting, I noticed a man sitting on a bench that was close to the shopping centre and felt I needed to go talk to him.

Even at that young age, I remember feeling "the nudge." I had no idea what I was going to say, but I knew God was with me and wanted me to be obedient, so I hopped out of the car. I walked up to the man, plopped myself down beside him, and asked, "Do you know Jesus?"

THINKING ABOUT THIS SITUATION TAKING PLACE NOWADAYS IS NERVE-WRACKING! BUT THAT WAS BEFORE CHILDREN WEREN'T LEFT ALONE IN VEHICLES AND NO ONE USED THE TERM "STRANGER DANGER."

He told me that he didn't, so I told him that Jesus loved him and had died on the cross for him. I think that was the extent of the whole conversation. I then said goodbye and got back into the car. I had—and still have—no idea what was going through his head or the conversation he might have had with his own family that night regarding this unusual encounter. I do know that God would've used those simple, uncomplicated words, spoken from a sincere five-year-old, to pursue the man's heart. God loved him so much that He set up a divine encounter just for him. Who knows what God had been stirring in his heart before I sat down beside him? God loved that man so much that he made sure someone spoke to him about Jesus.

That encounter was the beginning of my learning to respond to God's voice and the foundation of a faith and life filled with crazy miracles.

Years later, I had a similar encounter as I walked across the local high school track. I noticed an older man walking a distance in front of me and felt "the nudge" yet again. I quickened my pace until my steps joined his relaxed gait and I struck up a casual conversation. As we spoke, the Holy Spirit told me how much the Father loved this gentleman. I then relayed the message to him, straight from God's heart, and he gave his life to Jesus right then and there.

Immediately, his expression changed as he recognized his own value, years of disappointment and lack of self-esteem falling off his face. It was a profound moment for both of us; he was changed and I was deeply impacted by God's incredible love for people and His words that ring true for each of us... He leaves the ninety-nine to pursue the one (Matthew 18).

Twenty-five years later, the memory of that encounter suddenly popped into my mind; with it, came an urgency to pray for him. The intensity to pray increased throughout the day as I somehow understood he didn't have long to live. I was surprised thinking that he could still be alive because at eighteen years old, I felt that anyone over fifty years old was ancient.

I began praying, but was frustrated that I couldn't remember his name; I'd just recalled that it was unique. But God hadn't forgotten. I began looking all through the house, trying to find where I had journaled about that day, but couldn't find it anywhere.

That night, before I went to bed, I asked God that if He truly wanted me to pray for this man, then He needed to give me his name in a dream. I woke up the next morning and immediately recalled the dream I had in which God had spoken the name "Ripley." Yes, "Ripley, Believe It or Not!" I was ecstatic that God had answered my prayer and realized—again—He was leaving the ninety-nine to pursue the one. I prayed until I felt the urgency lift and was confident that God was with this man at the end of his life.

I love God's promise that He will never leave us or forsake us (Hebrews 13:5) and I'm certain that one day, I will be giving Ripley a huge hug in heaven.

Several years later, I found the story of Ripley, penned out in one of my many journals scattered in various places throughout my home, and felt the wink of heaven as I imagined Ripley in his forever home.

God used this ordinary island girl to be a little piece of the puzzle in one man's life. God continually uses our ordinary to reveal His extraordinary.

THE *Aroma* OF FRIED CHICKEN

No one needed a standard alarm clock on schooldays while I was growing up.

First came the piercing noise of the antique school bell at 6:00 a.m., jolting my siblings and me from our slumber, immediately followed by the thunderous sound of our mother's "Mighty Wurlitzer" organ reverberating through our house, shaking us out of our grogginess and propelling us to stagger up the stairs, blurry-eyed. The huge Leslie speaker was conveniently located above our rooms, pounding out the Christian happy-clappy songs of the 70s throughout the home.

Mom made the three-tier Wurlitzer come to life as Dad, on the piano across the room, tried to keep up with the way her fingers flew across the keys. Her feet were moving just as quickly, as though dancing across the pedals to a fully charged Riverdance performance. To this day, I've never heard anyone play the organ or piano like my mother. Many had marvelled at her ability to play by ear; she truly had an amazing gift!

Unfortunately, I wasn't as appreciative of those early mornings as I am now. I didn't understand the strong foundation being laid for me as I stood there, playing my tiny tambourine and singing my heart out to Jesus, with each lyric a solid principle of truth setting the unshakeable standard in my heart. The words of the songs were life to my spirit. I knew, as I was singing the words to "Jesus Loves Me" (Anna Bartlett Warner), that it was true, and that truth has been the anchor in every season of my life. Every song, no matter how simple, was etched in my spirit.

Our family travelled frequently to various churches and functions, where we sang and my dad preached. We were kind of like the Von Trapp family—minus the fashionable curtains and dancing through the mountains. (Mind you, we could be found swinging from the tops of huge fir trees on several occasions.)

I was the youngest of four and spent hours outside by myself. My tiny tambourine was my instrument and the tall trees on our thirteen-acre wooded property were privy to all my conversations with God. It was there where I learned to hear His voice as I tromped through our wooded property in my little black gumboots.

There were times when I would've traded being a PK in a heartbeat, just to be part of a "regular family." But now, as I look back, I'm so thankful for my heritage. Was it perfect? Heck, no—far from it! But now I see the gold mixed in with the dirt. The mud and sediment are always easy to see, but panning for gold takes time, and when you find those nuggets, they are valuable.

We all have a choice to make. We can focus on the mud— those crappy situations that can pop up and surprise us at any given moment throughout our day, painful memories randomly triggered—or we can decide to find the gold amid the pain and grief, recognizing the value it carries. If you focus your energy and attention on the mud, you will notice you'll get stuck there, unable to move forward in your life. Fear, anxiety, depression, and worry will be the sludge holding you captive to your painful memories.

I've seen so many people, myself included, anchored to the pain of their past, imprisoned in shackles of shame and torment, and held captive to it. It's become their identity.

We read in Psalm 40 as David pours out his heart and writes…

I waited patiently for the Lord; he turned to me and heard my cry. He lifted me out of the slimy pit, out of the mud and mire; he set my feet on a rock and gave me a firm place to stand. He put a new song in my mouth, a hymn of praise to our God. Many will see and fear the Lord and put their trust in him. (Psalm 40:1–3)

Isn't that amazing? Nothing we've gone through, no matter how terrible, can't be turned around for good. But we have a choice to make. Will we focus on the dirt or the gold?

Our songs of praise can rise up in the most difficult circumstance; they become a pleasing aroma to God. It's easy to praise God when we've had enough sleep and are in a naturally good mood; everywhere we look, we are filled with peace, joy, and happiness. What a world it would be if everyone liked us? No one was negative, everyone was polite, and checkout lines moved quickly. But guess what? It isn't exactly a sacrifice to sing a song of thanksgiving to God in the middle of your rose garden. The true sacrifice happens in the middle of the pain, hardship, misunderstanding, and uncertainty.

Many years ago, as I was in the car with my three young children, all singing along with a few children's worship songs, I thought I could incorporate a teaching moment. I decided to give them a mini lesson on praise and how God sees it as a pleasing aroma that rises up to heaven.

From the backseat of our minivan, my son Tyler's sincere voice interrupted my rambling monologue as he questioned, "I wonder if it smells like fried chicken?"

I must agree: fried chicken has a pretty amazing aroma (at least to me).

I'm certain that our praises in the middle of our heartache, uncertainty, sickness, setbacks, absolutely capture the heart of God—and might even smell like my grandmother's fried chicken to Him.

I'm reminded of a situation in which I wasn't sending up smells of fried chicken, but rather stinky garbage. I'm sure you can relate.

How many of you have been blindsided and didn't have the best response? I had a knee-jerk reaction to some very hurtful words someone had spoken about me. The statements came out of the blue; they were nonsense and outright lies. The words hit me with such impact that I felt punched in the gut. The shock gave way to hurt, which then made room for bitterness and anger—*ugly* anger. I sat on my couch, completely undone, and let loose some stinky garbage reactions.

My wise husband began praying quietly for a shift to take place in my extravagant self-pity party. His prayers were answered moments later, as I suddenly recognized I had fallen into the enemy's trap: choosing to be ticked off with this individual rather than choosing to pray for and bless them.

I began to shift my focus toward God's faithfulness and the truth He spoke about me. As I released a blessing over this person, my attitude immediately changed, as did the atmosphere in my home. The self-pity fog lifted, along with the hurt and anger. The tightness in my chest eased as God's peace settled over me.

I woke up the next morning to the hurtful words playing over in my mind and realized my battle wasn't over. I knew I needed to continue to walk in forgiveness or the situation would consume me in bitterness.

As I began to pray, the Lord immediately gave me a picture. It was the scene from *The Sound of Music* in which the seven children were performing a marionette puppet show for their father and the baroness. The kids were hidden from sight as they controlled the puppets by strings.

I instantly connected the dots and saw how the enemy was the puppeteer in my situation. He was hiding behind the scene, using this individual to attack me. It wasn't about the person and the hurtful words; rather, it was about the enemy controlling the strings, causing the attack against me. Once I saw the plans of the enemy and recognized it wasn't even about this other person, I was able to pray *with God's heart* for this individual. The enemy had been exposed, and I felt like doing a happy dance! Every targeted, hurtful word washed off of me.

In that moment, I was very much aware that God had my back. I then reached for my Bible and opened it randomly. I laughed as I looked down and read the word beneath my finger: "puppet." I didn't even know that word was in the Bible. Every trace of fear, anger, and anxiety that had wrapped around me had completely dissipated as I got ready for work.

I got into my car, and as I was backing out of my driveway, I began to belt out the lyrics, "This is how I fight my battles" (from the powerful song, "Surrounded" written by Ellysa Smith). I turned the radio on… silence. I found myself in an unusual "radio moment" of dead air space between songs. As though on cue, the singer's voice suddenly joined mine in perfect timing, singing, "This is how I fight my battles."

You can't make up these kinds of "God moments." I felt the approval of God as He confirmed that, once again, it never was my battle in the first place, but His. As I lifted up His name over the situation, He was taking care of the rest. I'm so thankful that this person didn't experience my knee-jerk reaction, but rather the extension of love from God who loved this individual! Over the course of the week, I was intentional in blessing this person and I watched as a miracle took place. There was a complete turnaround in our relationship and a genuine friendship formed.

So often, our immediate response is directed at the person hurting us, instead of at the real enemy. The person attacking us is not the enemy. The person attacking *you* is *not* your enemy! God has commanded us to love everyone. When we see each other through the lens of Jesus, He then gives us His love and grace. We will find ourselves being tested time and again as God wants to reveal our hearts to us. It's His grace that exposes the ugly inside of us. We realize we need His forgiveness and we also extend that forgiveness to others.

> *Finally, be strong in the Lord and in his mighty power. Put on the full armor of God, so that you can take your stand against the devil's schemes. For our struggle is not against flesh and blood, but against the rulers, against the authorities, against the powers of this dark world and against the spiritual forces of evil in the heavenly realms.* (Ephesians 6:10–12)

The simple truths I learned while singing in the early mornings of my childhood have become my wings to soar above every circumstance.

YOU
Belong

Insecurity was always lurking just beneath the surface, ready to take advantage of any mistake or perceived failure. I was as insecure as they came and struggled with being "enough."

The particular afternoon my older siblings decided it would be a great practical joke to tell me I was adopted didn't play out too well. As a seven-year-old, I bought it, hook, line, and sinker. I believed them, not just for the afternoon, but for several *years*!

My mother was fuming when she found out. I was inconsolable, blubbering for hours as she frantically tried to right the sinking ship. She even phoned some close family friends and asked them to tell me the truth, knowing I'd believe them; unfortunately, I did. When she handed the phone over to me, the male voice on the other end said, "I'm not sure if you've been adopted or not, but I know your parents love you!" This was not exactly the reassurance I was seeking.

My mom stood there stunned as I repeated to her his well-meaning reply. I handed the phone back to her, utterly gutted over my newfound "identity" (or lack thereof).

It would be several years until I believed the truth of who I was. The moment of revelation came as I was looking through family photos and couldn't deny the shocking similarities. Nope, there was never even a chance I was adopted. Same eyes, same smile, same laugh, and the nose—no denying the nose!

The prominent genetic facial trait became even more pronounced one gloomy afternoon at a funeral service. Friends and family had gathered at the little church to reminisce and say goodbye to my grandpa. We had just engaged in singing some of his favourite hymns when we were then asked to be seated. Positioned between my siblings, I sat down within the tight confines of the wooden church pew. I hadn't particularly paid much attention to the open casket in front of me while I was singing. I had my eyes closed for the most part (to be honest, open caskets have always creeped me out just a bit). But as I sat down, I found myself eye level with the rim of the open coffin. There before me, I beheld a nose... that family nose!

I wonder if Solomon had a similar experience, and that's why he wrote:

> *Your neck is like an ivory tower.*
> *Your eyes are the pools of Heshbon*
> *by the gate of Bath Rabbim.*
> *Your nose is like the tower of Lebanon*
> *looking toward Damascus.* (Song of Songs 7:4)

In that moment, I began to laugh. I tried to contain myself but to no avail. My siblings, privy to the same view, were hit with simultaneous humour; there was no hiding our front-row outburst.

Have you ever tried to hold back a guttural laugh? It's as though the quieter and more sombre the circumstance, the more boisterous the laughter. Controlling the embarrassing avalanche of emotion is next-to impossible. I tried to hold my breath, close my eyes, concentrate on anything but his nose, but nothing helped. Our row became the dance of synchronized shoulders, as wave upon wave of convulsive laughter rippled throughout the pew.

As I reflected on my family's many similarities, I was reminded of my relationship with my Heavenly Father and pondered whether I reflected His image.

So God created mankind in his own image,
in the image of God he created them;
male and female he created them. (Genesis 1:27)

I was nineteen, and no longer doubting my genetics. If the nose wasn't convincing enough, my laugh certainly tipped the scales into my believing that I belonged. My sisters and I were all blessed with the kind of laughter that can easily throw one's neck out of alignment as our gaze is forcefully thrust heavenwards. Our similar "snort and cackle" confirmed our family ties.

One morning, during my quiet time with God, I began to sing the song Abba Father." Tears streamed down my face as I sang the song to God from the depths of my heart. His love wrapped around me as the truth of each word confirmed that I belonged to Him. Suddenly, the Lord spoke to me and told me to turn to Galatians 4:6. Now some of you might already know what that verse says, but this nineteen-year-old certainly didn't. I struggled with memorizing John 3:16 then, and had no clue where certain scriptures were found. I was intrigued by the interruption from my melody and was curious about what I would find. I felt validation and the nudge of heaven as I read the words:

Because you are his sons, God sent the Spirit of his Son into our hearts, the Spirit who calls out, "Abba, Father." (Galatians 4:6)

I was completely undone in the moment, realizing I had just heard the Father's voice, telling me that I *belonged.*

A
Strange
VISITATION

"Guwd monin', Awnti Tammy!" came the sweet, barely decipherable words of my young niece, as she peeked around the corner and into my bedroom.

She was wearing a mischievous smile as her little feet pitter-pattered into my room and came to a stop beside my tall bed. Looking up at me with her adorable eyes, she waited for the inevitable "Aunty hoist"—a toss into the air and onto the soft bed.

Crawling to the oversized stuffed animal at the head of my bed, Bryanna would lay claim to the giant dog and we'd both enjoy our morning conversation and giggles. I loved our routine and was grateful for the opportunity to live with my brother, Jim, and his growing family.

I had a cute little room filled with organized chaos: an assortment of childhood memories, alongside current lifeguarding textbooks and resumes. It was a visible display of the confusion and uncertainty I felt as a twenty-year-old, navigating the transition into an unknown future.

Having just travelled and returned home from a conference, I was happy to be back in familiar surroundings. It had been a disappointing experience, as I had spent most of my time in the hospital and couldn't participate in any weekend sessions. I had waited in an emergency room due to a ruptured eardrum from an ear infection and was desperate for relief from the incredible pain. Sent home with antibiotics and painkillers, I was extremely exhausted from lack of sleep and looking forward to sleeping in my bed.

The deep sleep lasted only a few hours; suddenly, I was awakened in the middle of the night from a fitful dream. Sensing a "nudge from heaven," I glanced toward my bedroom door and noticed an unusual figure. I sat up in bed, a little drowsy from the medication, and asked, "God, what are you trying to show me?"

My words pierced the darkness as my eyes tried to adjust to the departing shadow.

Convinced I was having a heavenly encounter, like the one Paul had in Acts 27, I stumbled out of bed in search of the figure who had quickly exited upon hearing my spoken question. I was certain I was about to have a "Moses experience"—perhaps I'd look out the living room window and see a burning bush.

> *For God's angel visited me last night, the angel of my God, the God I passionately serve. He came and stood in front of me.* (Acts 27:23, TPT)

Determined not to wake my young niece or her sleeping parents, I tiptoed through the hallway, but found no one in our quiet house. Disappointed, I returned to my bed, and pondered the strange encounter before drifting back to sleep.

The next morning, I awoke to the smell of freshly brewed coffee wafting under my bedroom door. I followed my nose to the kitchen. Smiling from her highchair, Bryanna was excited to see me, since we had missed our morning routine. I grabbed some breakfast and joined my brother at the table and noticed he was acting a little odd. Then, I suddenly remembered my strange visitation in the night and excitedly told him about the angel I'd briefly seen. I explained I hadn't got an answer yet from God regarding what He was trying to show me.

Failing to celebrate this holy experience with me, Jim made me vividly aware that not all things are as they appear (or, in this situation, "disappear"). With a condescending tone, he retorted, "Well, that angel robbed our home last night!"

Standing with my mouth agape, he explained that my sister-in-law's purse had been stolen, as well as a bucket of ice cream from the freezer. I'm not sure what type of thief steals dessert as he escapes, but this one had a hankering for some strawberry ice cream while heading through the mudroom and past the deep freeze.

My appetite suddenly vanished as I sat at the table, staring at my uneaten breakfast. Still trying to process the news, I heard an abrupt knock at the front door as Jim explained to me that the police had been called. He told me I would be asked a few questions, since I was the only eyewitness.

Given his facial expression, the uniformed officer wasn't expecting my honest recount of my night's adventure. My thoughts that I had seen an angel made it apparent that he would never forget this particular interview. Guaranteed, his investigation would be a conversation in the police detachment that afternoon.

Reflecting, I am amazed at the "nudge from heaven" that caused me to wake up and speak those words out loud and unafraid! Had I known it was an intruder, I would've screamed and then… who knows? I don't want to imagine what could've happened! My words spoken to God scared the intruder and caused him to leave without causing harm to me or the rest of my family farther down the hallway.

I'm certain he'd never been involved in a B&E quite like this one! And I'm assuming, God gave him his very own "nudge" down the road.

WHEN GOD
Shows Up

OLD VW VAN + YOUNG PEOPLE + JESUS = MIRACLES

The vibrant colours of tulips indicated that seasons had shifted in Holland, as pristine fields of the Dutch bulbs filled the horizon with a beauty difficult to rival.

It was spring 1990 in the Netherlands. I with part of an organization called YWAM (Youth With A Mission) and our school was one of hundreds around the globe with the intent: To Know God and Make Him Known.

Our tight-knit community of nine students had flown in from various places around the world, and congregated in Ede, the beautiful city in the centre of the Dutch-speaking nation.

Flying to the European country had been on my radar for several years after God had spoken to me and told me it would be an important part of my life. I was excited to see the dream become a reality as I was walking in the Lord's promise to me.

One sunny afternoon, our small ragtag team of world changers packed up overnight bags and embarked on an adventure. Cruising on the left side of the road in our cool, blue VW van, we headed north. Picturesque landscapes of canals and flat fields dotted with unique windmills, whizzed past our windows.

We travelled to a northern town where we were billeted out to several accommodating families. I was paired with another team member to a wonderful family who opened up their hearts and home to us.

After an exhausting day of street preaching using an interpreter, I couldn't wait to fall into bed that night. With thoughts of the eventful day playing out in my mind, I dozed off into a deep sleep. I woke up as the sun was creeping around the curtains and shining right in my face.

Something was feeling a little off. I had a twinge of panic as I felt my throat constrict and I struggled to breathe. A strange sensation spread across my face; when I tried closing my eyes, they felt stuck.

I quickly jumped out of bed and ran to the bathroom. I was stunned as I saw my reflection in the mirror. I literally saw my face transforming before my eyes; the panic morphed into full-blown fear. My face looked disfigured. Not only was my face misshapen, but my eyeballs had a cloudy, white film spread over them, and I was unable to move them side to side or up and down. It was as though someone had poured glue into both eyes and they were literally stuck.

I splashed cold water on my face, but when my throat continued to constrict even more, I quickly ran downstairs for help. The mother in the house where I was staying gave me an antihistamine and sent me outside for fresh air. She had quickly assessed the situation and immediately knew I was having a severe allergy attack.

I had been struggling with cat allergies, but nothing on this large scale. I was definitely reacting to the houseful of adorable felines they had in their home—all of whom had, unfortunately, taken a strong liking to me.

Once I stepped out of the cat-friendly environment, my breathing improved and I realized I wasn't going to die.

Of all the mornings for this to happen, I thought. It was Sunday morning and our team was scheduled to be the guest speakers at the morning church service. The conversation playing out in my head sounded something like this:

"Crap, I look freaky! There's not a chance that I want to be seen by *anyone* right now, let alone an entire congregation! Jesus, help!"

I'm not sure about you, but sometimes, when I have a running monologue in my head, it helps me process the situation. Unfortunately, there are many times when the words swirling in my head escape and become audible to the startled people within earshot. My internal dialogue left me with no alternative but to join the rest of the team for the morning service. There was no way I was staying back in the cat-infested home.

Pulling into the church parking lot, I stepped out of our billet's car into the bright sunshine. At least I had a decent excuse for wearing shades. With my sunglasses firmly in place, I joined the rest of my team before heading into the sanctuary. I had already determined that my sunglasses would stay on my face throughout the entire service, no matter *how* ridiculous I looked.

I spent most of the service slouched in the pew, my hand resting at the side of my face, shielding me from any curious stares. As our leader was wrapping up his message, I felt myself breathe a sigh of relief, knowing everyone would soon be dismissed out into the glorious spring day. I was hopeful I'd be able to escape the claustrophobic surroundings without anyone seeing my face disfigured from the extreme allergic reaction.

My sigh of relief was soon replaced with terror. The leader called our entire team to the front to pray for people—for healing, of all things.

Are you kidding me? I can't go up front wearing sunglasses! I silently screamed to myself in utter desperation. I felt like a deer in the headlights. I wanted to be obedient, but I was more concerned about what others thought of me.

Recognizing the pride in my heart, I sheepishly removed the sunglasses and made my way up to the front. I felt insecure and vulnerable as I turned and faced the large congregation, even as I knew I didn't speak their language. Before I knew it, a middle-aged woman approached me, wanting to receive prayer for healing. How was I to pray for someone needing healing when I desperately needed healing myself? The words from 2 Corinthians had never been more applicable, as the Lord reminded me that He was my strength.

> *But he said to me, "My grace is sufficient for you, for my power is made perfect in weakness." Therefore I will boast all the more gladly about my weaknesses, so that Christ's power may rest on me. That is why, for Christ's sake, I delight in weaknesses, in insults, in hardships, in persecutions, in difficulties. For when I am weak, then I am strong.* (2 Corinthians 12:9–10)

Once I realized this woman didn't speak a word of English, I relaxed and began to pray what I felt God telling me to pray. Every trace of anxiety slipped away as I prayed God's heart over this beautiful woman. She began to cry as I spoke in tongues over her and her situation and then the Lord told me to hug her. As I reached out to her, she walked into my embrace; as we hugged, the Holy Spirit came upon both of us with such force that we literally staggered back from each other. It felt like I had been struck by lightning. The electricity that shot through both of us was so intense that we just stared at each other in awe. We began to laugh as we experienced the power of God touch our bodies. I became unglued—quite literally, as I realized my eyes and face were instantly healed.

And to think, I nearly missed out on such an incredible miracle.

God doesn't look at our ability, but our availability. Make yourself available and watch what He will do!

He said to them, "Go into all the world and preach the gospel to all creation. Whoever believes and is baptized will be saved, but whoever does not believe will be condemned. And these signs will accompany those who believe: In my name they will drive out demons; they will speak in new tongues; they will pick up snakes with their hands; and when they drink deadly poison, it will not hurt them at all; they will place their hands on sick people, and they will get well." (Mark 16:15–18)

I KNOW *the Plans* I HAVE FOR YOU

DECEMBER 1, 1997

"Push!"

That was the only word that pierced through my intense focus. I was determined to "redeem" myself from my previous labour experience two-and-a-half years earlier, and did not want a repeat occurrence of an attending nurse yell at me, "Shut up!"

That experience had left me feeling completely humiliated once I had come to my senses, and the barrage of "F-bombs" quickly dissipated into the rehearsed Lamaze breathing.

There's something incredibly humbling when a sweet elderly lady, a patient in the hospital, wanders past your delivery room as your highly charged words at uncontrolled volume reach her ageing ears. Then, just imagine, a few hours later, strolls into your wing of the hospital and smiles at you, tenderly asking, "Was that you, dear, who had a baby this morning? I heard you."

Great.

In that moment, I was certain I'd never felt this mortified in my entire life and I wished the hospital bed would just swallow me up so I didn't have to look into the eyes of this sweet woman. And to think that birth had been called a "textbook delivery." What's "textbook" about squeezing my husband's hand as my nails dug hard into his flesh? Greg calmly endured my madness as he looked down at his hand to see if there was any blood and then heard me say, through gritted teeth, "P-R-O-M-I-S-E M-E I W-I-L-L N-E-V-E-R H-A-V-E T-O G-O T-H-R-O-U-G-H T-H-I-S-A-G-A-I-N!"

I didn't release my grip until I saw him nod his head in agreement.

That was the summer of 1995. That delivery was its own story, as our middle child, Jordan, was born on the seventh day, in the seventh month, weighing seven pounds, seven ounces in the seventh hour of the morning.

Then, an unfamiliar doctor, with the name Dr. Grace, delivered our son. You know heaven has winked at you when your son is "delivered by Grace." True to his name, he wasn't even fazed by my loud, not-so-polite language gushing out of my mouth uncontrollably. When I sheepishly apologized to him a few hours later, he assured me it was okay. I felt his grace extended to me and I was reminded of how much God always extends grace to us. God truly doesn't gasp, shake his head, and rub our faces in our shortcomings; instead, He tells us that His power is made perfect in our weakness.

Let's go back to Monday, December 1, 1997. I was determined not to have a repeat "out-of-control" experience. I wanted to prove to my husband—and mostly to myself— that I could deliver this baby without freaking out. It had been two hours of proper breathing through each contraction and I was proud of myself for staying focused. I was exhausted, but excited, when I made it through the transition stage without losing my concentration.

Our regular doctor walked through the doorway and looked ready to deliver my baby. He had told me in one of my previous check-ups that he would be hanging up his scrubs from delivering babies. After a lengthy career in being a part of the birthing room experience, he was going to enjoy not being disturbed from his sleep at all hours of the night. This delivery was to be his second to last.

However, it wasn't until the following day that he explained that his decision to walk away from deliveries was also based on not wanting the stress and responsibility of complicated births. Little did he know, this would be one such birth. As he entered the room, the nurse updated him with the progress of the last two hours and within minutes, I was given the green light to push. But what should have been a fairly short pushing stage, turned into a three-hour nightmare.

My doctor's voice cut through my own thoughts again: "Push!" I rallied my strength to bear down but felt the exhaustion of being in the final stage of pushing for three long hours. I was impressed with myself for not screaming like my previous labour experience and felt like I had done an incredible job of staying focused as I concentrated on my breathing. I was determined not to have any elderly lady comment on my flowery vocabulary after the birth of this baby. But even with my focus and concentration this time around, I became increasingly agitated; I knew something was desperately wrong.

I tried voicing my concerns between each contraction: "This baby is stuck!"

My motherly instincts heightened as I recognized my strength was rapidly decreasing. My husband and a close family friend were standing on either side of my bed, encouraging me to stay strong, but my body was losing its ability to push. I had become too weak to continue. I tried one last time to convince those in the room that something was wrong; what should've been a total of two hours had turned into five hours without any progress.

"Please, listen to me, something is wrong!" I cried out in one last desperate attempt. "I delivered my boys and it wasn't like this!"

As if on cue, my baby's heart rate immediately showed signs of distress and the atmosphere notably shifted in the room. It became a race against the clock to deliver this baby. I was quickly given an episiotomy and forceps were used in the effort to get my baby out of danger. Concerns were being voiced as both doctors (I hadn't noticed earlier that the local pediatrician was also in the delivery room with us) were now fully aware that this baby was not positioned properly, and with every contraction of the past three hours, this little one had been pushed up against my pelvis with no possibility of being delivered without help.

I found it a little strange that the pediatrician was also in the room with us but didn't give it too much thought. I found out later that he was asked to be present in the delivery room because a few weeks prior, things weren't going as planned. I had been in my doctor's office for my routine checkup, when my doctor realized that my baby hadn't yet turned and was stuck in the breech position. With only a couple of weeks to go, this could have posed a risk to the baby and to me.

He had immediately sent me to the hospital to have an ultrasound to confirm the position of my baby. He informed me that if the baby were in the breech position, I would be scheduled for a C-section. This news upset me, and my pregnancy hormones wanted to send me into a tailspin.

Memories of a previous miscarriage jumped to the forefront of my mind and left me feeling vulnerable as I drove the quick seven-minute drive across town to the hospital. During that short drive, I prayed and asked God to turn my little munchkin around because I did not want a C-section. This was going to be our last baby and I didn't want to go through surgery.

While praying, I suddenly felt the baby flip as I was driving. It was the craziest feeling! The ultrasound, thirty minutes later, confirmed my baby's acrobatic move; I was ecstatic! However, I didn't know that the delivery was still deemed high risk and my doctor had wanted his colleague to be present in case of any complications.

The final push was a blur, as the intense pain gave way to relief and my little girl was quickly whisked away. Yes, my little girl! Astonishment and absolute delight gripped me; I turned to Greg, and saw joy mingled with concern on his face. Brooke became the focus of the medical staff as they moved her to another area in the room to run various tests and make sure she was okay.

As I lay there, utterly exhausted, a wave of nausea washed over me and I knew I needed a bucket. The pediatrician was about to leave and head out the door. Just before he disappeared around the corner, he glanced back toward me.

"I don't feel very good," I whispered weakly. Observing that my doctor was occupied with sewing up my incision, he clomped back into the room in his cowboy boots. I'll never forget staring down at his preferred footwear and hearing the sound they made echo throughout the room. He stood beside me and placed the blood pressure cuff around my arm.

"Seventy over twenty!" His words commanded the attention of all present medical staff and a practiced swiftness surged into the room. Immediately, my baby girl was hurriedly passed into my husband's arms, as all of the attention turned to me. Someone pushed a button on the wall, prompting the emergency code ringing throughout the hospital, and suddenly the room was a flurry of activity. The crash cart was called and the space was filled with every available doctor and nurse.

I honestly don't remember all the details, but my husband has relived the traumatic experience many times over. It was at that point when I literally felt my life slipping away. Extremely relaxed, I was ready to drift off to sleep.

Before that day, I'd always been anxious at the thought of dying, and had struggled with a fear of death, but in that moment, I had no fear. I looked up at the pediatrician standing directly over me, and with little energy left, asked him: "Am I going to die?"

"Stay with me, Tammy, stay with me!" he kept repeating.

The atmosphere in the room was urgent yet the voices and sounds became muffled as I felt myself detaching from the room.

Suddenly, the Lord's clear, authoritative voice pierced through the frantic activity in the room. The doctor's words took a backseat as the loud, audible voice of God filled the entire room. It's difficult to articulate this experience and what God's voice sounded like. The commands of the doctor trying to keep me alive were muffled as I recognized the authority that suddenly captured my full attention.

"I know the plans I have for you, plans to give you hope and a future and not to harm you!" God declared.

It's as though time stood still in that moment; a hush fell over the urgency in the room. Only one voice commanded my attention, and with it, a supernatural peace flooded my entire body. Instead of panicking or becoming overwhelmed that I had just heard the voice of God, I was completely calm and knew I was going to be okay.

I looked toward my husband as he held our beautiful daughter and I could see the tears sliding down his cheek; his face gave away the fear and anguish he was battling. Only later did he explain the emotions at war within him: He was finally holding the daughter he had always longed for, yet fully aware he was losing his wife.

"Don't go to sleep! Don't close your eyes!" encouraged a young nurse in a purple shirt, standing over my left shoulder. She repeated this urgently yet steadily.

Everything in me wanted to drift off to sleep, but somehow, in my hazy state, I was aware I needed to follow the medical team's continual prompts. I locked my gaze with the young nurse and drew what little energy remained to keep from closing my eyes. There was no anxiety or worry. No panic or fear for the future, just peace—incredible peace. In that moment, I was living in the words found in Isaiah 30:15: "*In quietness and trust is your strength.*"

I had complete confidence in what God had spoken to me. It wasn't until later that fear and anxiety came knocking at my door. That's when I had to remember the words the Lord spoke to me and declare them over every anxious thought. I have spoken the words found in Jeremiah 29:11 (*"For I know the plans I have for you," declares the Lord, 'plans to prosper you and not to harm you, plans to give you hope and a future'*) over numerous situations in my life. God has had to remind me many times since that experience of the words he spoke to me on that snowy winter's day in 1997.

Several hours later, I was stabilized enough for the nurses to try and move me out of the delivery room. Not being aware of the actual amount of blood I had lost, they sat me up and transferred me to a wheelchair. As I was being taken down the hallway, everything went black. I passed out with my eyes still open and my body slid toward the floor. The nurse made a quick assessment of the scene playing out before her, noticed the telltale signs Greg was exhibiting of shock, and sent him away in search of pillows.

Meanwhile, thousands of miles away in Florida, there was a godly woman who was praying for me. Catherine, my best friend's mother, had been given the nudge from heaven to pray for me the previous night:

"Pray for Tammy! Pray for Tammy!"

She prayed throughout the night. Early the next morning, she phoned her daughter, Ruthann, to find out what was going on with me, explaining to her the urgency of what she was feeling. Ruthann, unaware of the unfolding events, quickly phoned Greg to see if I had delivered the baby. Greg confirmed what God had shown her mother the night before, explaining the scary complications and asking for continued prayer on my behalf. During that window of time, Greg placed a few strategic calls to people whom he knew would intercede on our behalf. To know we weren't alone in this battle was the strength my husband needed.

Greg and I wouldn't find out until the following day of how close to death I had come. My postpartum hemorrhage had caused me to lose over half the blood in my body; I spent the next ten days recovering in the hospital. It was during the course of my hospital stay that I became incredibly aware of God's protection over Brooke and me. I was visited by both of the attending doctors the following day and filled in on some of the details, the most significant of which was the fact that I was alive without having had a blood transfusion. I had survived a "Class Four" hemorrhage and all I had been given was IV fluids. I was told that, had they known the amount of blood I had lost, they would have given me a transfusion. My doctor was extremely thankful for the outcome of his second-to-last delivery and now, more than ever, he was ready to hang up his scrubs and forceps. We, especially my husband, were all amazed and extremely thankful for the outcome.

A few weeks later, I took a thank-you card and some homemade cookies to the pediatrician who was part of my miracle. Had he not turned around and clomped back into my hospital room in those memorable cowboy boots, I'm certain I wouldn't be telling this story. I told the pediatrician about my experience that day when I heard God's voice.

He listened intently and nodded his head, saying, "I believe it! We were close to losing you and weren't aware of how much blood you had lost. There's no other explanation."

As I write and recount this miracle, I'm once again undone and brought to tears at God's love and faithfulness. His promises are trustworthy and He's never failed me.

I've had the opportunity to share my story countless times over the years and I never lose the wonder.

"Never be afraid to trust an unknown future to a known God."[1]

---

[1] Corrie Ten Boom, *Clippings from My Notebook*. (Thorndike Press, 1983), page 35.

I
Love
MY HOUSE

AN ORDINARY SPRING DAY

March 27, 1998, was a relatively mild spring day in our small Canadian community in B.C.

It had already been an extremely long, northern winter, and my children were eager to get out of the house and enjoy the long-awaited sunshine and warmth. My two sons, Tyler and Jordan, had enjoyed five cold, snowy months, playing with the kids in the neighbourhood. They learned how to skate on our communal front yard ice rink on which my husband and some friends worked tirelessly. Many late nights, I watched Greg from the kitchen window as he sprayed down the rink with the garden hose. He spent hours trying to make the perfect rink for the kids. Nothing says "true Canadian town" more than outdoor hockey rinks!

This particular morning seemed like the perfect day to take my boys and my four-month-old girl, Brooke, to the park. The boys needed to burn off some pent-up energy, and my daughter and I would enjoy some fresh air. I was excited to let them try out the new addition to the children's playground. The anticipation of spring was in the air as Tyler and Jordan eagerly waited to play outside without the burden of bulky snow pants and winter gear that comes with freezing cold weather. I managed to get all three children buckled into our family van and headed out for a morning of fun.

When we arrived at the local park, I noticed two other moms with their children, enjoying the first signs of spring on the snowless playground. My boys quickly scrambled out of the van while I worked at getting Brooke's infant car seat pulled out of the vehicle. Grabbing the diaper bag and container filled with snacks, I headed after my excited crew. I decided to keep Brooke in her carrier, as she was content for the moment, and it freed me to push Tyler on the swing as well as chase Jordan around the colourful maze of new equipment.

As my oldest child made friends with one of the children, I walked to the nearest picnic table and placed Brooke's carrier on top so she could watch her older brothers' flurry of activity. Within twenty minutes, Jordan had wandered over to the nearby softball fields where Greg and I had played countless innings of slo-pitch. The wide-open space allowed me to keep an eye on him, as he was about a hundred meters away.

While I was keeping tabs on all three children, I noticed Jordan had bent down close to a two-foot post in the ground. I figured he was playing in the dirt, using sticks and rocks as cars. As I prepared the snacks at the picnic table, I kept looking over at Jordan and noticed that he hadn't moved from his spot for about fifteen minutes. He remained in the crouched position with his head down.

Jordan, at that time, almost three years old, was extremely shy, something he might have picked up from his older brother.

Both boys had a habit of putting their head down, chin nearly to chest, when being spoken to by an unfamiliar adult, as they would try to turn "turtle-like" by disappearing into an invisible shell. It was a habit Greg and I were trying to address by having them look into the eyes of the people who were speaking to them. It seemed that my sons were destined to go into their adult years becoming acquainted with people's shoes.

After watching Jordan crouched down for such a long period of time, I decided to go check on him to see what he was doing. As I began walking toward him, he slowly stood up and headed in my direction. I can still hear his sweet little voice ask me as I approached him:

"Mommy, why was that man talking to me?"

I was keenly aware that there were only three families in the park, ours being one of them, and no men in the mix. I knew for certain that no one had physically come close to my son and I immediately knew that he had just experienced a heavenly encounter.

Remaining as calm as I could, I asked him, "What man?"

He pointed to the corner entrance and said, "There he goes!" It was obvious by his response that he was actually seeing somebody. I realized this was a remarkable moment and I wanted to use it as a teaching opportunity on the supernatural and how natural it actually is. I had always wanted the supernatural to be an everyday occurrence in the lives of my children, and my prayers were being answered right here on an ordinary spring day.

It suddenly dawned on me why he had been crouched down for so long with his head touching his chest; someone had been talking to him that entire time. As excited as I felt, I tried to contain myself, which anyone who knows me would agree that's no easy task! I wanted Jordan to know that this experience was just a normal, natural occurrence in the life of someone who loves Jesus. I had prayed for each of my kids while they were in my womb that they would know God and walk in the same signs and wonders in which the apostles in the Bible had walked, but even greater. I wanted the truth found in John 14:12 ("...*whoever believes in me will do the works I have been doing, and they will do even greater things than these...*").

"What did he say to you?" I began inquisitively.

I was a little deflated when he responded with, "I dunno."

"What was he wearing?" I asked next, a bit absentmindedly. *My son just spent more than fifteen minutes talking to an angel and I asked what he was wearing?* I thought to myself, shaking my head.

Regardless of my random question, Jordan replied, "A red shirt."

"Was he nice or mean?"

I was relieved with his response: "Nice!"

"What did he say to you?" I repeated.

"He said the ice is bad!"

"The ice is bad?" I repeated, confused. "What ice?"

I held his hand as we walked back to the spot where he had spent fifteen minutes. To my horror, I saw that Jordan had been crouched down in the middle of an apparent party hangout. People had been gathering there over the winter months to hang out around a fire and drink. There were broken glass bottles everywhere. Jordan, thinking they looked like the giant icicles hanging on our house, had decided to put the broken glass in his mouth. A man had appeared to him, took the glass out of his mouth, and told him, "The ice is bad."

I was shocked, feeling a knot in the pit of my stomach, as the gravity of nearly losing my son settled in; however, the awesomeness of having an angel show up to rescue him trumped my fear and horror.

I then bombarded my middle child with every question imaginable because I wanted to know everything that happened. But after the countless questions, all Jord chose to tell me was, the man was wearing a red shirt, he was nice, and the ice was bad.

After arriving back home, I was excited to tell Greg what had happened, but I also told him how disappointed I was because I couldn't extract any more information from my tight-lipped son.

My husband offered some wise advice: Maybe we weren't supposed to know everything that had been said and it was just between this man and our son. Greg figured that if we were supposed to know, it would happen when Jordan wanted to tell us. That made sense to me if we were talking about a teenager, but not an almost-three-year-old! But I listened to my husband and was content and thankful, knowing my family had just narrowly escaped incredible grief. I had a little boy who was still alive and he had just experienced an incredible supernatural encounter.

Over the next couple of weeks, I was continually reminded of God's protection, and although my heart was extremely thankful, I had told only a few close friends about the encounter. They agreed with Greg and felt like I didn't need to bring it up with Jordan again. Although I never brought up the incident again with my son, I did pray and ask God that if I should know what had been said that morning, Jordan would eventually tell me.

Two weeks later, when I walked into the boys' room to put away laundry, Jordan was on the floor playing with his cars. He looked up at me and asked, "Mommy, why was that man talking to me?"

I looked around the empty room, wondering if the same man had appeared, and asked him, "What man?"

"The man at the park."

I was stunned that he was bringing up the incident because he had said absolutely nothing about it for two weeks. Again, I was trying to hide my excitement as I asked the exact same questions I had at the park; I was also curious to see if he'd change his answers.

"What was he wearing?" I asked.

"A green shirt."

I was confused, but just then he pointed to a ball across the room and asked, "Mommy, what colour is that?"

I looked over at the ball. "Red."

"No, he was wearing a red shirt!"

My insides were bursting, as I knew he was remembering his encounter "an eternity" ago. My prayers were being answered in this precious moment between the two of us, as I was being given a window into the day at the park.

I then asked a question I hadn't even thought to ask at the park.

"Was it Jesus, or an angel?"

"Jesus," he replied without hesitation.

I was ecstatic but I didn't want this moment to pass without learning what else was said during that encounter.

"What did he say to you?"

"The ice is bad," he answered simply as he continued playing with his toys.

"Jordan, what else did he say to you?" I asked, barely containing my emotions.

He paused for a moment, and then said, "He loves His house."

"He loves His House…" I repeated those words out loud, more to myself than to my son, and then asked him, "Where's His house?"

I thought he would say "heaven," but he stunned me with his answer: "The church."

The words taken right out of scripture hit me with such force that I knew my son had experienced an encounter with the Risen King!

I ran throughout our house, yelling, "He saw Jesus; he saw Jesus!"

So much for staying calm.

> *But Christ is more than a Servant, he was faithful as the Son in charge of God's house. And now we are part of his house if we continue courageously to hold firmly to our bold confidence and our victorious hope.* (Hebrews 3:6, TPT)

Over the years, I have thought about that day at Kinsmen Heritage Park. Yes, Jesus literally saved my son that morning, which is amazing in and of itself. But God reminded me of my prayer to Him, asking to disclose anything in that conversation I needed to be made aware of. I feel a responsibility as I realize, I am the mama's voice and feet to this encounter; my son wouldn't have remembered the simple, yet weighty words spoken to him all those years ago on his own.

> *This is what the Lord, the God of Israel, says: 'Write in a book all the words I have spoken to you.'* (Jeremiah 30:2)

What is so important about the church that Jesus came to rescue and tell a two-and-a-half-year-old how much He loves it? I know my son didn't get into some theological or philosophical debate with the Lord about what church is or isn't. In the same way, we need to take Jesus' words at face value and understand the simple, yet weighty truth: Jesus Loves His House.

CONNECTING THE DOTS

Several years later, I found my journal entry for March 27, 1998, and was overcome as I relived that day. As I read the encounter out loud, my attention was immediately drawn to the name of the park: Kinsmen Heritage Park. How had I never connected the dots before? In the Bible, Jesus is referred to as our Kinsman Redeemer, a male relative who had the responsibility to act on behalf of a relative who was in trouble, danger, or need.

I suddenly became so excited as I felt the nudge of heaven. Grabbing my Bible and dusting off my old dictionary, I embarked on a word Easter egg hunt. The search certainly didn't disappoint and was more satisfying than any chocolate delectable I'd ever eaten.

This is what I found:

Kinsman[2]: "a man who belongs to the same family as someone else."

Both the one who makes people holy and those who are made holy are of the same family. So Jesus is not ashamed to call them brothers and sisters. (Hebrews 2:11)

Redeemer[3]: "a person who redeems; Jesus."

Synonyms for "redeemer" include deliverer, rescuer, saver, and saviour. The root meaning in Hebrew for the word "redeem" is "goel." The "goel" was the closest male blood relative still living. There were certain obligations that were expected of him toward his next of kin. God is the Goel of His people, His church, His house. He's our redeemer, our kinsman-redeemer.

---

[2] *Cambridge Dictionary.* (Cambridge, U.K.: Cambridge University Press, 2020), s.v. "Kinsman," https://dictionary.cambridge.org/dictionary/english/kinsman.

[3] *Merriam-Webster Dictionary.* (Merriam-Webster, Incorporated, 2020), s.v. "Redeemer," https://www.merriam-webster.com/dictionary/redeemer.

Goel[4]: "Redeemer, Reclaimant, especially a next of kin upon whom according to ancient Hebrew custom devolved certain family rights and duties including… the redemption of a relative in helpless circumstances."

Goel[5]: (Hebrew: לאוג, lit. "redeemer"), in the Hebrew Bible and the rabbinical tradition, is a person who, as the nearest relative of another, is charged with the duty of restoring the rights of another and avenging his wrongs."

In the Book of Isaiah, God is called the Redeemer of Israel, as God redeems His people from captivity; the context shows that the redemption also involves moving on to something greater. In Christianity, the title *goel* is applied to Christ, who redeems His believers from all evil by offering Himself as the Paschal Lamb.

I love that it says, "nearest relative." Here's a neat thought: Christ is our nearest relative.

But now, this is what the Lord says—he who created you, Jacob, he who formed you, Israel: "Do not fear, for I have redeemed you; I have summoned you by name; you are mine. When you pass through the waters, I will be with you; and when you pass through the rivers, they will not sweep over you. When you walk through the fire, you will not be burned; the flames will not set you ablaze. For I am the Lord your God, the Holy One of Israel, your Savior… (Isaiah 43:1–3)

Heritage[6]: "property that descends to an heir; birthright."

[4] *Merriam-Webster Dictionary*. (Merriam-Webster, Incorporated, 2020), s.v. "Goel," https://www.merriam-webster.com/dictionary/goel.
[5] *Wikipedia*. (Wikipedia, 2020). s.v. "Goel," https://en.wikipedia.org/wiki/Goel.
[6] *Merriam-Webster Dictionary*. (Merriam-Webster, Incorporated, 2020), s.v. "Heritage," https://www.merriam-webster.com/dictionary/heritage.

For those who are led by the Spirit of God are the children of God. The Spirit you received does not make you slaves, so that you live in fear again; rather, the Spirit you received brought about your adoption to sonship. And by him we cry, "Abba, Father." The Spirit himself testifies with our spirit that we are God's children. (Romans 8:14–16)

Jesus appeared to my son as his Kinsman Redeemer. He not only saved his life from danger but also had a fifteen-minute conversation with him! It is the words spoken to Jordan that have commanded the attention of this mama's heart: "I love my house."

Throughout scripture, the church is referred to as God's house, and I believe we are at a strategic point in history where we will see the fulfillment of heaven's destiny for His church.

This is what the Lord Almighty says: 'In a little while I will once more shake the heavens and the earth, the sea and the dry land. I will shake all nations, and what is desired by all nations will come, and I will fill this house with glory,' says the Lord Almighty. 'The silver is mine and the gold is mine,' declares the Lord Almighty. 'The glory of this present house will be greater than the glory of the former house,' says the Lord Almighty. 'And in this place I will grant peace,' declares the Lord Almighty." (Haggai 2:6– 9)

Get ready! Prepare yourself! His glory is coming!

I get fired up reading Haggai's words of the promise to God's church. The Lord reassures us, wanting us to know that in the middle of the shakedown, He's not going to leave us high and dry. In fact, it's quite the opposite! He's warning us about the shaking that needs to come, in order for His glory to be revealed in us, His church. And in the middle of the chaos and the crazy, we have access to peace. God tells us in Haggai 2:9 that He will *grant* peace.

When the shaking comes, we will have access to peace. It will be ours when we ask. But I feel like God is saying to us that the world will need His peace like never before. They will be looking for the authentic peace that only Christ can give.

Arise, shine, for your light has come,
and the glory of the LORD rises upon you.
See, darkness covers the earth
and thick darkness is over the peoples,
but the LORD rises upon you
and his glory appears over you.
Nations will come to your light,
and kings to the brightness of your dawn.
(Isaiah 60:1–3)

Remember, He loves His house!

*My family sang at various churches and events. My siblings
and I were often asked to sing "Jonah and the Whale."*

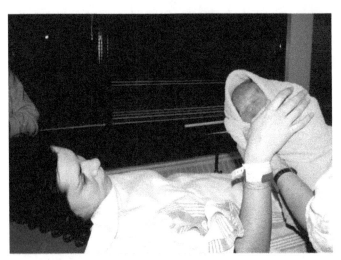

*Seeing my precious daughter for the first time several hours
after the harrowing delivery.*

Tyler, Brooke, and Jordan a few months after the visitation in the park.

Our family playing together on the same ball team
—Greg, Tyler, Brooke, Jordan, and one proud mama!

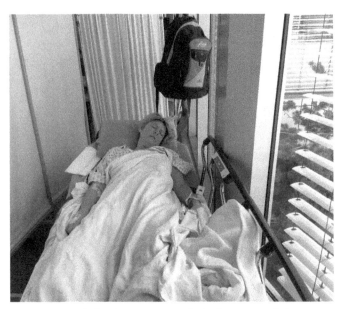

Moments before hearing the words "Pulmonary embolism!"

Surrounded by my prayer warriors
—my dear friends and pastors Brian and Leah Robertson.

Having my family all together after my embolism, filled my mama's love tank. Each moment together is a precious gift.

My imaginary Charlie's Angels *convertible Ford Mustang…
now vintage.*

This is what redemption looks like.

When tattoos become your testimony…

ALL BECAUSE
OF A
Dream

Just one week into September, a lot was going on in our busy little family's home. The shift from warm summer days to the slight autumn chill had arrived as the cooler air rolled in without apology. My oldest child, Tyler, had just started first grade and we were all transitioning into the new situation of his going to school for full days. Life was just a touch fuller, but it remained relatively peaceful on the home front... up until I had a dream.

I suddenly awoke, my racing heart loudly interrupting the quiet morning. Shaking uncontrollably, I became aware of my tear-drenched pillow and felt a sense of heightened panic the dream had caused.

It was only 5:00 a.m., but I didn't hesitate to call my husband's name over and over.

"Greg! Greg! Greg! Wake up!... please wake up! We need to pray!"

Words gushed out of me as I desperately tried to articulate the terrifying scene still playing through my mind. I was completely aware that it had only been a dream, but I was even more aware that our six-and-a-half-year-old's life was at risk. I knew we needed to pray.

I pled with God to protect Tyler and while I knew it wasn't God's plan that any harm should come to him, I couldn't shake the images replaying in my mind...

I was walking on a famous suspension bridge with my family and friends. At one point, I casually turned to check on the whereabouts of my kids and noticed my oldest son trying to get a better view of the river that rushed a few hundred feet below. Panic gripped me as I called out to him to back away from the low railing; it was extremely dangerous and he was leaning too far over.

Before I could formulate my warning, he fell. He was gone.

Sobbing, I crumpled to my knees. The horror of witnessing his death was too much for me to bear. People screamed all around me and everyone responded differently to the situation. Some rushed over to me, while others ran off the bridge, toward the place where he'd landed.

I couldn't bring myself to look; I knew he was dead.

In that moment, I came face to face with the deep, guttural pain of losing a child. It was overwhelming. My body convulsed in sobs and a hollow formed in the pit of my stomach, trauma wrapping around me like a lead blanket.

I slowly stood to my feet as his body was brought to me. I looked down at my son's flat, lifeless form, but instead of intense grief, a sense of authority and righteous anger overcame me. The deep sorrow immediately fell off me as I began to speak life over my son. I didn't care who was watching me or what they thought.

"In the name of Jesus, you will live and not die!" I declared loudly.

As I spoke those words, air began to blow inside of him, as though someone was blowing into a rubber dish glove. Each flattened part of his body filled up with the breath of God.

After that dream, I spent the entire day interceding on my son's behalf and kept declaring life over him.

Over the next few weeks, I felt ill and could barely eat, as the burden of the dream hadn't lifted. I found myself constantly praying for him. Every time I thought of the dream, I felt sick to my stomach and started declaring life over the spirit of death.

A few weeks later, we had a wonderful visit from my mother-in-law, who flew north to spend a few quality weeks with us. Her visits were always extra special, as she had such a close relationship with us and her grandchildren. Every so often, when her Gramma Bupa's love tank was running on empty, she'd make the long trek north and get a refill.

This particular visit was especially helpful, as she helped look after our kids while Greg and I were both at work.

One evening, the smell of Gramma's home cooking welcomed me as I opened the front door. I was greeted with,

"Hey, come quick and look at the TV!" I heard her call with excited urgency from inside the house.

Instead of putting down my bags and taking off my coat, I hurried up the stairs and as I came around the corner, I saw her and my husband staring at the TV. I knew something significant had happened.

Just then, I heard the reporter say, "The baby survived the fall from the suspension bridge!"

My mouth fell open as I stood in shock.

I immediately turned to Greg. "That's who I've been interceding for these past two weeks. It wasn't for Tyler!"

Shock, joy, and tears overcame me as I stood staring at the images on the screen and reading the headlines, many of which referred to the "miracle baby." This precious little one had survived a fifty-metre fall out of her mother's arms from the exact same suspension bridge that had appeared in my dream… a bridge I had never been on before.

I continued following the story over the course of many months, and one day, I felt a nudge from heaven to contact the mother. This family had just experienced extreme trauma and I strongly believed they needed to know the love of the Father.

The process to contact them was easier said than done. This was at a time when the Internet was in its early stages and not every home was equipped with a computer. However, my husband worked with computers and after some searching, excitedly handed me a phone number—the mother's.

I had no idea what I was going to say without sounding phony or ridiculous. I was supposed to phone a complete stranger to tell her that God loves her so much that He gave me a warning dream about her baby falling off of a huge bridge, so I prayed, and they survived?

I figured the worst thing she could do was hang up on me, so I dialed the long-distance number. I nervously waited and wanted to hang up as soon as I heard the woman's voice on the other end: "Hello."

I pushed fear aside, said a silent prayer under my breath, and forged ahead, waiting the entire time to hear the dreaded *Click*. I finished my entire spiel without losing her. Success! By the end of our conversation, we had even set up a date so we could meet her and her children. It was a thirteen-hour drive, but well worth it. This woman needed to know how much she was loved!

The day we met was one I'll never forget.

She came to the door and laughed. "You're not what I expected!"

She didn't elaborate but I'm sure she was expecting to see some crazy lady standing in her doorway. I guess that was somewhat of a compliment telling me I was relatively normal looking.

We ended up having a wonderful visit as our children played together and I told her how much Jesus loved her and her family. She allowed us to pray for each of them and my heart was instantly connected to theirs. As I held her little girl who had miraculously survived the fall, I was incredibly grateful to be woven into the mosaic of their lives. It was a powerful moment and I was deeply thankful for a loving God who prompted me to pray for this precious gift, all because of a dream.

We both had dreams," they answered, "but there is no one to interpret them." Then Joseph said to them, "Do not interpretations belong to God? Tell me your dreams." (Genesis 40:8)

"In the last days, God says, I will pour out my Spirit on all people. Your sons and daughters will prophesy, your young men will see visions, your old men will dream dreams. Even on my servants, both men and women, I will pour out my Spirit in those days, and they will prophesy. I will show wonders in the heavens above and signs on the earth below, blood and fire and billows of smoke. The sun will be turned to darkness and the moon to blood before the coming of the great and glorious day of the Lord. And everyone who calls on the name of the Lord will be saved." (Acts 2:17–21)

YOU
DID NOT
Kiss BAAL

Sifting through the new shipment of fitness merchandise, I meticulously organized and priced the various products for display at my workplace. The successful gym was a hotspot for sports enthusiasts in the small Alpine-themed community, especially through the winter months. It was a great place to dryland train for hockey players, curlers, downhill and cross-country skiers, runners, cyclists, and anyone needing the extra resistance training required for their upcoming sport.

Completing the pyramid display of protein powder, I turned just as the front door beside me swung open and in walked *Joe (*not his real name). I had never actually spoken to him before, but I always had a strange sense that he was trying to avoid me. Well, there was no avoiding me this time; we practically collided.

Making the most of the awkward encounter, I greeted him with a friendly hello and he used the opportunity to introduce himself. First, he asked if I was a Christian (I nodded) and then told me that he was a Satanist high priest. Not exactly a typical everyday introduction! Maybe he was going for the shock factor, since he probably already heard through the tightknit community that I was a Christian.

Unfazed by his bizarre introduction, I continued the conversation without missing a beat and purposed in my heart to pray for him.

Little did I know, I was about to enter the biggest test of my life.

Test me, O Lord, and try me, examine my heart and my mind. (Psalm 26:2)

Undaunted by his disclosure, I was determined to be kind and extend God's love and grace to him. With a sense of excitement, I looked forward to what I felt was a divine setup.

Over the next several weeks, *Joe visited the gym more frequently. Instead of avoiding me, his demeanour changed and we began to engage in meaningful conversations that would invariably circle back to my faith. I pulled no punches when telling him how much God loved him because my heart wanted everyone to know about God's love. He would always respond with a laugh and continue his workout, and I would continue to pray.

After a few months of daily interactions, something in our relationship began to change. I can't tell you the moment I noticed the shift, as it was a slow fade. I became increasingly more concerned with my body image and what I looked like when getting ready for work. My thrown-together wardrobe took a bit more thought and the extra time in front of my mirror should have been a wake-up call.

My eight-year marriage began to suffer as I began to spend more and more time at the gym. Times together with my husband and three children became sporadic at best. My family took a backseat to my workplace and intense fitness regime. I received a steady stream of praise from *Joe and fellow gym members, who continually complimented me on my physique. I became driven in my newfound fitness challenge, each compliment fueling an insatiable fire within me. I couldn't walk past a mirror without striking a pose and noticing how toned I was becoming and how my muscles were taking shape (this was before the era of selfies and social media).

Yearning for approval from those in my fitness sphere, I gradually pulled away from my home life and the predictable mom routine. I escaped daily family obligations, which in the past had fed my soul. My heart became increasingly numb, as choices I made no longer triggered my conscience.

I had entered the darkest season of my life as temptation increased and my personal time with God decreased.

> *When tempted, no one should say, "God is tempting me."*
> *For God cannot be tempted by evil, nor does he tempt*
> *anyone; but each person is tempted when they are dragged*
> *away by their own evil desire and enticed. Then, after*
> *desire has conceived, it gives birth to sin; and sin, when it*
> *is full-grown, gives birth to death.* (James 1:13–15)

Eight years earlier, on the sunny morning of December 21, 1991, in front of family and friends, Greg and I committed our lives to each other and to God. Our marriage had been established on love, faith, honesty, and integrity. I just assumed our "I dos" would last forever.

We had cultivated an incredible relationship and established a family environment of love and laughter. Hours were spent together camping, biking, swimming, playing at the park, and celebrating birthdays and random calendar events like Groundhog Day (Greg's favourite). We loved exploring trails and skipping rocks in rivers. If someone had been a fly stuck in our family van on one of our countless road trips, you would've heard singing, laughing, and bad dad jokes, and then more laughing. We were inseparable! But after years of being married to my best friend, our vows were about to be put to the ultimate test.

The shift was subtle; by the time I recognized my attraction to *Joe, it was already too late. Each time he entered the gym, I felt inexplicably drawn to him.

Have you ever walked into a spider's web? You don't see it until it's too late and it sticks to you; the more you twist, turn, and even run, the more entangled you become, as it has already attached itself to you. I became entangled in a web of sin that followed my every move. The first place the web attached itself was to my mind; my thoughts were continually bombarded day and night and had become a battlefield.

I never imagined I would ever be tempted to walk away from my husband and my three young children, but before long, *Joe and I were planning out an affair. I was in such a dark place and felt numb toward the truth in which I had anchored myself since I was a little girl.

> *God's will is for you to be set apart for him in holiness and that you keep yourselves unpolluted from sexual defilement. Yes, each of you must guard your sexual purity with holiness and dignity, not yielding to lustful passions like those who don't know God... For God's call on our lives is not to a life of compromise and perversion but to a life surrounded in holiness. Therefore, whoever*

rejects this instruction isn't rejecting human authority but God himself, who gives us his precious gift—his Spirit of holiness. (1 Thessalonians 4:3–8, TPT)

One afternoon, while I was home doing the umpteenth load of laundry, I had a "God moment." The oppressive battle in my mind cleared momentarily and I felt a tangible fear for my hardened heart. I had strayed so far away from the plumb line of truth. Suddenly, I felt the nudges of heaven calling my heart back to God's love. Throwing myself onto my knees on our basement floor, I cried out to God for help. I asked Him to take away the feelings I had for this man.

I love the Lord, for he heard my voice; he heard my cry for mercy. (Psalm 116:1)

A few days later, my desperate plea to God was answered with an unexpected phone call. I was working an evening shift at the gym when the phone rang. I answered and was surprised to hear my sister's voice on the other end. Kim lived a thirteen-hour drive away, and although we had occasional phone conversations, she had never called me at work.

My response to her voice was a little hesitant, as I thought she might be calling with some bad news. It wasn't long until I figured out the motive for her call. With no preamble, she simply asked, "What's going on?"

Let me explain something about my oldest sister: She hears God and most of our phone conversations revolved around God and what He was up to in our lives. The tone in which she asked the question gave me no margin to skirt around the issue. I knew that she knew! I wasn't surprised, just annoyed. Since I was at work, I told her I'd call her back when I got home.

Driving home after my shift, I wrestled with the thoughts of being completely honest with her, knowing the hidden places of my heart would be exposed. But I decided to be vulnerable and tell her the truth, as I figured she knew it anyhow.

I got home and tucked myself away from listening ears and made the inevitable call.

Jumping in with both feet, she again asked, "What's going on?"

But instead of waiting for my reply, she charged full steam ahead, filling me in on the uncanny events leading up to her inquiry. Unbeknownst to me, I had various people praying for me. Just that day, on three separate occasions, friends had approached her and asked about me, and one of them didn't even know me. They all had the same questions: "Is your sister okay?" ... "What's going on with your sister?" ... "I've been praying for your sister!"

Let me emphasize the fact that we didn't live close to each other. In addition to the thirteen-hour drive between us, there was a two-hour ferry ride. It's not as though her friends were spying on me.

Her words felt like a *thwack!* from heaven, instead of the familiar nudge.

With an air of defiance, I answered, "I'm about to leave my family and have an affair."

It was as if I had been given a truth serum and couldn't hold back my words.

"Oh no, you won't!" she immediately answered, even more defiantly, and then proceeded to prophesy God's call and destiny over me and my family. Her words were fully charged and demanded a response.

The turmoil raging through my heart was palpable as my sister came alongside me in the battle and covered me with her shield. I wanted to lash out but knew I needed to heed her advice and tell my husband everything. Her phone call was strategic as she stormed the gates of hell on my behalf.

The first step toward change came when I was honest with the women with whom I was in leadership (I was still involved in church leadership during this struggle). I disclosed to them everything, still not entirely convinced the affair wasn't going to happen.

Instead of judgment, I was met with love, grace, and mercy. Sitting there with my heart completely exposed, I felt the Father's love begin to soften every hardened place. My confession brought light into the darkest place where my sin was hiding. One might think that by confessing where I was at, I would have felt relieved to have exposed everything that had been hidden, but my conscience was still numb. The war certainly wasn't over; however, the battle line was about to be drawn in the sand.

Later that week, I was working a closing shift at the gym. I was only minutes away from locking the door when *Joe walked up to the counter. Panic gripped me as I was confronted with two choices and hadn't firmly committed to either.

He leaned in, and barely inches from my face, asked, "What do you want to do?"

Unable to articulate my thoughts due to the intense battle warring in my heart, I waited until I found my voice. With a strength that I hadn't felt for months, my response shocked even me. I pulled away from his potential kiss and said firmly, "You need to leave."

"Are you sure?" he asked, unwilling to give up so easily.

I nodded my head. "Yes," I quietly replied.

Without saying another word, he turned and left the gym.

The flickering light of the T.V. greeted me as I walked in the front door. I said a quick hello to Greg and tiptoed past the rooms of my three sleeping children. Shutting my bedroom door behind me, I fell to my knees yet again. I was broken and empty as I let the tears fall, wondering if I would ever feel the presence of God again. My thoughts were immediately answered as I felt Him turn toward me. This time, there was a gentleness in the nudge, prompting me to open my Bible. My heart was racing as I let the pages fall open, my gaze going to where my finger was randomly pointing. This is what I read:

Yet I reserve seven thousand in Israel—all whose knees have not bowed down to Baal and all whose mouths have not kissed him. (1 Kings 19:18)

I began to weep as I felt the pursuit of the Father and realized he had left the ninety-nine to come for me.

The moment I had been dreading had come. I could no longer ignore the nudges from heaven prompting me to be completely honest with my husband and tell him the truth. Struggling for the right words, I forged ahead, not knowing how he would respond. Would my confession end our marriage?

It felt as though I was standing on a platform of a high diving board looking over the edge. I did *not* want to jump! I knew as soon as I started to speak, there was no going back; I was in unfamiliar territory.

The words felt foreign on my tongue, as though spoken by someone else, but I continued with my honest confession. The impact on my husband's heart escaped as silent tears rolling down his cheek.

Bracing for his response, I couldn't have anticipated what happened next. Displaying what love looks like, he stood up and pulled me in tight to an undeserved embrace. My heart was wrecked as I felt unmerited grace wrap around me. In that moment, I knew God had not forsaken us and He would put our broken pieces back together.

Bringing to light and exposing my hidden sin was the first step to restoring our relationship. It took months of navigating through the twists and turns of my confession, but we both recognized the value of fighting for our marriage and our children. There was a daily struggle to take every thought captive because the feelings I had for *Joe didn't just vanish overnight. But I became intentional in my effort to please God, and in my weakness, He was my strength.

> *For though we live in the world, we do not wage war as the world does. The weapons we fight with are not the weapons of the world. On the contrary, they have divine power to demolish strongholds. We demolish arguments and every pretension that sets itself up against the knowledge of God, and we take captive every thought to make it obedient to Christ.* (2 Corinthians 10:3–5)

Over the following weeks, I began to feel again. My hardened heart began to soften, but in the process, shame became relentless in its pursuit of me. It became my biggest enemy through our restoration, as it attacked the truth of what God thought about me.

How many of us, while growing up, heard a parent, a teacher, or someone in authority say, "Shame on you"? Those three words have carelessly been thrown around and do not come from the heart of the Father. Shame camouflages itself as being part of repentance, but it has nothing to do with being sincerely repentant. It is rooted in fear and is a liar! Shame has destroyed relationships and has claimed countless lives.

PRIDE IS AN INTERESTING THING; IT BLURS THE LINES AND MASKS THE CONDITION OF OUR HEARTS.

Many years have passed since this part of my journey took place. Since then, I have seen countless marriages face similar situations, but sadly, many of these relationships have imploded and the families are left completely shattered. The devastation that is caused in the wake of our pride leaves a ripple effect on our families.

Our loved ones are then left in the waves of rejection, abandonment, bitterness, anger, jealousy, anxiety, and hate.

The highway of the upright avoids evil; those who guard their ways preserve their lives. Pride goes before destruction, a haughty spirit before a fall. (Proverbs 16:17–18)

You might be in a broken relationship because of unfaithfulness. I want to speak hope to you and your situation. God can restore your heart. It doesn't mean the road ahead will be easy, but healing will happen when you surrender to God. When you raise your white flag, you will see God fight for you and your family.

In my distress I prayed to the Lord, and the Lord answered me and set me free. (Psalm 118:5, NLT)

So, if you think you are standing firm, be careful that you don't fall! No temptation has overtaken you except what is common to mankind. And God is faithful; he will not let you be tempted beyond what you can bear. But when you are tempted, he will also provide a way out so that you can endure it. (1 Corinthians 10:12–13)

Invariably, all of us will be tested. Our own free will and response will be a window into our hearts and reveal what's hidden.

THE
Missing
PIECE

Have you ever worked tirelessly on a puzzle, only to realize, near its completion, there's a missing piece?

It's such a deflating moment. It changes the entire look of the puzzle and your eyes always seem to gravitate to the missing space. You search everywhere: on the couch, under the couch, behind the couch, under the coffee table, in every nook and cranny, even inside the gross vacuum bag. But it's gone. Vanished! Missing with the likes of the infamous single socks. What would've been a satisfying moment has now been replaced by a feeling of frustration.

What if *we* were the missing piece in a puzzle, a massive puzzle—the world's largest seven-and-a-half-billion-piece people puzzle? Each of us has been designed to be connected with others—interlocked. Your life and story are integral pieces to the outcome of a beautiful mosaic. What would happen if we hid from who we've been called to be?

Let me tell you a story that happened a few years ago about a beautiful mosaic into which I was privileged to be woven.

Glancing up from my work as I heard the back door open, I smiled at the familiar client as she entered. As I observed her sad demeanour, my friendly greeting sounded hollow as she stood directly in front of me. I noticed her anxious expression as her eyes filled with pooling tears. She told me that she would be needing to take some time off and that I wouldn't be seeing her for a while. I stepped toward her to surround her with a hug and my heart felt her pain that was visibly spilling onto her cheeks. More tears came as she explained that she was heading to the hospital to say goodbye to her husband. Both she and her son had conferred with the medical team and had made the difficult decision that this would be the day to take him off life support.

I didn't pretend to know what she was going through but I certainly had empathy for her broken heart. Feeling the "nudge of heaven," I told her I would be praying for a miracle and asking God to intervene on her husband's behalf. She immediately stepped back from our hug and looked at me with a quizzical expression, thanked me, and left.

Throughout my shift, I continued to pray for this precious man—that God would reveal Himself to him. As the day progressed, I found my prayers begin to shift as I focused more toward this dear woman and her son and the grief they must have been experiencing. Little did I know it would be several months until I was told the full story of what happened that day.

Glancing up from the scattered papers on my desk, a feeling of déjà vu engulfed me as I noticed the familiar woman standing in front of me. This time, however, her countenance from our previous encounter had shifted considerably, and a smile spread across her beautiful face as she greeted me. I tentatively asked how she was doing.

"You'll never believe what happened that day after I met with you!" she spoke excitedly, filling me in on the miraculous details of her husband's heavenly encounter.

Immediately upon her entry through the familiar doors of her husband's hospital ward that day, she was met by an eager nurse running toward her, who announced, "I was just with your husband, and asked him to squeeze my hand if he could hear me—and he did! Your husband is not braindead!"

My precious friend was glowing as she continued to share her story. Her husband had been in a coma after suffering a medical incident that left his brain deprived of oxygen for an incredible amount of time. After many weeks of lying unresponsive in a hospital bed, the doctors informed her that he was braindead and, unfortunately, nothing more could be done for him. They encouraged her to take him off of life support, explaining that even if he did come out of the coma, he would never be the same person. He would be a vegetable—unable to walk or talk.

Remaining steadfast in her response to the unhappy doctors who tried to persuade her to reconsider, her decision was validated shortly after.

She remembered the words I had spoken to her and was curious about the turnaround of his condition. When he awoke from his coma, she asked him if he had experienced anything while in that state. His response caught her off guard:

"I heard a voice tell me that my time on earth wasn't finished!"

Jumping around ecstatically, I gave her a huge hug as I celebrated this amazing story with her. She laughed and tried calming my exuberant outburst so she could continue sharing the entire miracle. She proceeded to inform me that not only was her husband walking and talking, but he had also just renewed his driver's license.

Several months later, I noticed a happy couple sitting near the window of the local coffee shop. Recognizing the familiar face, I made a beeline toward them and introduced myself to her husband, The Miracle Man.

I'm so grateful I responded to the "nudge of heaven" and had the chance to agree with the plans and purposes of God for someone else's loved one. I was given the opportunity to be interlocked with the pieces in this family's puzzle.

Each one of us will experience incredible miracles as we respond to heaven. Together, we make the most beautiful mosaic when we choose to connect with the people around us.

Great are the works of the Lord;
they are pondered by all who delight in them.
Glorious and majestic are his deeds,
and his righteousness endures forever.
He has caused his wonders to be remembered;
the Lord is gracious and compassionate.
(Psalm 11:2–4)

HON,
I'VE BEEN
Misdiagnosed

Intense pain pierced my left side as I made another concentrated effort to take a deep breath. I was desperate for air but felt anxious for the tremendous discomfort I knew it would create.

I had already spent the past few weeks in an unbalanced rhythm of inadequate breathing, each breath lacking a normal intake of oxygen. The sleepless nights of constant discomfort were taking a toll and making it difficult to think rationally. I was exhausted as I attempted to continue working as a gym manager. Between greeting clients, I sat on the floor, hiding behind the counter gasping for air as I mustered my strength to push through the sharp pain. Desperately needing my depleted lungs to fill with air, I was instead left with the sensation of breathing through a tiny straw.

One afternoon, feeling defeated after a difficult shift at work, I stepped inside the front door just as the torrent of tears came. Struggling to hold myself up, I leaned against the window, trying to find the most comfortable position to relieve the piercing pain under my ribs. I felt my husband's hand gently touch the small of my back and heard his voice amp up with authority as he called out to God. He had been my prayer warrior since the pain had begun several weeks earlier and he didn't relent to pursue heaven on my behalf.

He saw how the constant pain was affecting me and felt lost with his ability to help. I had barely eaten in the past few weeks and had become extremely weak. I could only nibble tiny amounts, and even then, the pain would intensify and become unbearable.

"Hon, I've been misdiagnosed," I managed to gasp quietly between short breaths. "I need to go to the hospital!" A flash of frustration crossed his face. He had seen my health deteriorate over three weeks and knew I had already been admitted twice in one day at a local clinic a few days earlier. I had driven myself to an urgent care clinic, only to be released and sent home with a prescription for ulcers.

His anger was palpable as we drove past the clinic and continued the thirty-minute route to the nearest hospital. He wasn't upset at me but rather at the ridiculous ulcer diagnosis. His usual calm demeanour gave way to frustration as he sped down the highway. A police car in the rearview mirror caused him to ease off the gas pedal, which only increased his frustration. I was half-tempted to flag down the police so we could get there more quickly; instead, I remained hunched over in the passenger seat, struggling to breathe.

Three weeks had been far too long in this condition and I was beginning to realize that something was seriously wrong. The blood pressure cuff tightening around my arm seemed to squeeze out some memories of the past few weeks, giving me the clarity to connect some important dots.

A few weeks earlier, I had been at work, when I suddenly experienced a strange sensation travel through my chest. Sweating intensely, a wave of nausea washed over me and sent me running to the bathroom. Kneeling in front of the toilet, I hoped no gym members within earshot could hear me heaving on the other side of the door.

What the heck just happened? I asked myself. An internal conversation ensued as I tried to figure out what was happening inside my body. A fearful fleeting thought of pregnancy crossed my mind, but at fifty years old, I was sure that wasn't the case, and quickly ruled that out with a sense of relief.

Trying to determine the cause of my abrupt sickness left me with unanswered questions, especially since the feeling lifted shortly after. I emerged from the washroom a bit clammy and shaky, but was able to continue to work. I was feeling completely normal by the time my boss got to work about fifteen minutes later and I filled him in on my strange experience.

That "strange experience" was now in the spotlight as I was being bombarded with questions from the hospital's triage nurse. I explained to her that I had been admitted into a local clinic earlier in the week—twice. Both times, I was told I had an ulcer and was sent home with a prescription for an applicable medication but found no relief.

Within minutes, I was placed in a wheelchair and whisked down the corridor to the radiology department. The skilled technician promptly jumped into her role and took the necessary images that would hopefully give some much-needed answers. Apologizing profusely for the pain the awkward positions were causing me, she asked me to take a deep breath and hold. Once done, she quickly placed a warm blanket over my shaking body and sent me with the waiting porter for more tests. It didn't take long for me to realize I wouldn't be sleeping in my own bed that night.

The doctor gave the nurse my prescription for pain and informed my husband and me that more tests would be conducted in the morning.

Shortly after midnight, my situation became worse as the pain intensified. I asked Greg to start praying because I felt a spirit of death enter my hospital room. As my eyes were closed, I saw our neighbour who had died two years earlier. He was standing in the doorway. My husband's response was swift as he fervently began to pray and speak life over me.

If you ever want to see an immediate response from someone, tell them you can see a dead person standing close to them. It's astonishing how quickly they respond!

Greg quickly sent an urgent email to our church's prayer chain coordinator explaining the situation, asking others to join in immediate prayer. She responded within minutes and explained that God had just woken her up and prompted her to check her email. That stirred faith in my husband that this battle was the Lord's and He was already alerting others to pray. Within hours, his prayer request had reached family and friends around the globe.

I found myself praying throughout the night in between my groans. I knew that God was with me and His presence was greater than the spirit of death I had felt enter my room. I even sent Greg home, knowing I was going to be okay.

The next morning brought with it a battery of promised tests. The doctors and specialists left no stone unturned as they sought to confirm what they each suspected. It didn't take long before the answer came, dismissing the previous ulcer diagnosis. The medical team had deliberated over X-rays, ultrasounds, and bloodwork results.

The doctor standing at the foot of my bed signalled Greg over and questioned if I had been in a car accident. Noticing my confused expression, he then remarked, "It looks as though you've had a blow to your chest."

Looking toward Greg, I asked, "Is that why the nurse asked me if I was safe?"

"You have a pulmonary embolism," the doctor continued. "Your lung has partially collapsed and there's blood pooling at the bottom of it."

A pulmonary embolism? I had no idea what that meant, but I knew it wasn't good.

Without any hesitation, my dad, who had been standing at my bedside overhearing the diagnosis, began to pray. I was grateful he and his wife were there in that moment, as I was trying to wrap my head around the doctor's words.

Fighting back tears, his voice broke several times as He asked God to heal me and spare my life. Reminding God of His promises, his prayer was heartfelt but charged with faith. Standing just behind him was Leah, one of my dearest friends. She placed her hand on his back and joined the fervent prayer with faith and authority. As a pastor, she knew the importance of joining with my father's prayer to declare life and healing over my body.

My husband, still standing at the foot of my bed, spoke in hushed tones with my stepmom and the words "blood clot" jumped out at me like a bold neon sign. Up until that moment, I had no idea what a pulmonary embolism was—or how serious, for that matter. But when the nurse gave the first blood thinner injection into my abdomen, scenes from various emergency room television shows came to mind.

Just as I was sensing the gravity of my diagnosis, the brakes of my bed released as the porter whisked me away to a scheduled ultrasound. The test on my legs was to determine the origin of the clot. The voices of my loved ones faded into the distance as I was wheeled away from my support system. The stark hallway echoed the wheels of my bed as the bright lights overhead whizzed past in an orderly sequence. The sounds and smells of the hospital heightened my emotions of vulnerability and helplessness. A sense of being alone crept over me, causing familiar tears to trickle on to my hospital pillow. I knew there was nothing I could do but trust God.

Straining to see the images on the monitor, the sonogram easily could've been an abstract painting in an art exhibit. I certainly couldn't make sense of what the ultrasound technician's eye was trained to detect.

After her thorough examination, no clot was found, which meant there would be more tests. In the meantime, I was reunited with Greg and the rest of the crew and moved into a new room, but this time, sharing space with another patient. The tight accommodation had a thin partition separating me from my new roommate, so I never had an opportunity to see her face before my sleep-deprived body responded to the pain medication.

I woke up in the wee hours of the morning, momentarily forgetting about my hospital surroundings. My nose was alerted to a distinct smell, so I groggily rolled over, trying not to tangle the IV line inserted in my arm. Opening my eyes and scrunching up my nose, I struggled to take a deep breath and the pain that pierced my side jolted me awake. I tried adjusting my vision to the dim lights in the hallway and the darkness in my room by blinking several times. My brain was having difficulty comprehending the haze of smoke coming from the entrance of my hospital room.

But there, in the doorway, stood my roommate, a lit ciga-rette in one hand. Noticing I was awake, she began to speak with me and express her disgust of the poor quality of service in our "hotel." As her free hand waved expressively around our "all-inclusive resort," the fingers of her other hand held the cigarette to her lips, with puffs of smoke circulating in the sterile air.

In disbelief, I reached for the nurse's call button but couldn't find it anywhere in the dark surroundings. Hoisting myself out of bed, I held onto my IV pole for support, held my breath, and shakily walked through the grey cloud lingering in the doorway. Flagging down the nearest person, I gasped as I tried to call out, "Help!" The janitor looked at me, confused, but then noticed the woman flicking ashes onto the floor, and suddenly clued in. Within moments, my depleted lung was rescued as the situation was swiftly dealt with by bewildered medical staff. I felt as though I was being filmed for one of those reality T.V. shows that surprise unsuspecting people in ridiculous situations.

After sincere apologies from the nurse, he checked my stats and administered more pain medication, which helped me once more drift off to sleep. The next time, however, instead of waking up to cigarette smoke, I awoke to my roommate sitting at the foot of my bed, staring at me. Feeling like I was in some thriller movie, I uncomfortably tried sitting up to back away from her intense stare. For a fleeting moment, I felt annoyed and wanted to ask her to move, but then I felt the "nudge of heaven."

Recognizing the divine setup, I said, "Good morning!" and asked her a few personal questions. Knowing God's heart for this precious woman, I felt heaven's wink throughout our conversation. I was so thankful I didn't respond with a knee-jerk reaction, but instead, was able to share the Father's love for her before being wheeled off again for another test.

The different names of the tests were beginning to blur together but the CT pulmonary angiography was an experience in and of itself. As the warm sensation of the contrast dye coursed through my body, I began to have a quiet conversation with God and reminded Him of the words tattooed on my arm (Jeremiah 29:11).

Vivid memories of Brooke's birth flooded my thoughts along with the familiar Bible verse and peace settled over me as I remembered His promise. If God was for me, who could be against me? I had people from all over the world praying on my behalf and fighting this battle with me.

> *"For I know the plans I have for you," declares the Lord, "plans to prosper you and not to harm you, plans to give you hope and a future."* (Jeremiah 29:11)

Settling into a new ward, I was extremely grateful for my room with a view. I felt so blessed as my bed was next to the window overlooking the incredible island mountains and ocean. Perhaps my ex-roommate was correct in her assumption that we were staying in an all-inclusive resort. Finding myself as the youngest in my new room and most likely, the entire floor, I tried to cheer the elderly patients. I was able to pray for and love them as they each recovered from their individual hip replacements and various surgeries. I certainly didn't want to waste a perfectly good opportunity to share God's love.

After getting a selfie with my favourite nurse, she proceeded to give me my scheduled blood thinner injection. I was given a shot twice a day into my now-bruised abdomen and was informed I would be on blood thinners for the rest of my life. Those words sounded overwhelming, but I knew God had something up His sleeve!

I had a choice: I could focus on the unknown and give fear the driver's seat, or I could trust God and stand on every promise

He had spoken to me since I was a little girl. I chose the latter. Plugging my headphones into my iPad, I spent hours listening to songs that declared the goodness of God. I quietly sang the words through each laboured breath and felt the promise of Isaiah 35 come to life in a tangible way.

Strengthen the weak hands, steady the shaking knees! (Isaiah 35:3, CSB)

One song rose above the others, like it had been written specifically for my circumstance ("Great Are You Lord," written by Leslie Jordan and David Leonard [of All Sons and Daughters]).

Nearly a week into my hospital admittance, surrounded by several visiting family members, I was visited by one of my many physicians. He glanced around and smiled at those standing near my bed before stepping in closer for a more private conversation.

My sister, Jody, a former paramedic, stayed close to be an extra set of ears for the latest update.

Pausing a moment and looking as though he didn't know how to proceed, he forged ahead and said, "Well, you have us all baffled!"

Not knowing what he was about to say next, I braced myself for the diagnosis.

"You're the talk of the hospital right now," he went on. "You have all of the doctors and specialists confused. We just finished meeting together and, well, your blood clot has disappeared."

Seeing my perplexed look, he continued, "The diagnosing specialist is good at what he does. He doesn't make mistakes. He knows what he saw. We can see the scar from where it had been, but it's gone, and they don't just vanish like that. We don't know what happened!"

I began to laugh as I replied, "I do! God healed me!"

He responded with a nervous chuckle, but listened as I continued. "I've had people all over the world praying for me," I explained. "Seriously. God healed me."

"All over the world?!" he repeated emphatically, clearly confused.

"Yes, *all* over the world!"

At that point, he didn't deny the miracle, but instead, informed me that the tests showed I was still dealing with a partially collapsed lung with pooling blood. The good news between his declarations was the fact that I wouldn't be on blood thinners for the rest of my life.

To place an exclamation mark at the end of his bedside meeting, the friendly doctor revealed to me that a small portion of my lung tissue had died, but since it was minimal, it shouldn't pose a risk down the road. Apparently, I was in the six percent of Canadians who were placed in the category of experiencing an unexplained pulmonary embolism. Regardless of the reason, I was just thankful I wasn't in the high percentile of people who died because of one.

My hospital experience came to an end one week after admittance. Enduring countless injections, scans, X-rays, and blood tests, I was discharged with the knowledge that heaven had, once again, intervened.

WE HAVE A
Choice

I recently survived a major home renovation and I'm still standing. I thought I had survived unscathed, but what's a home renovation without some mishaps? Aren't those mishaps the ones that build character?

The problem is, the "character" that surfaced wasn't exactly something to write home about. It got downright ugly; *I* got downright ugly! And not an ugly you can mask and pretend you're still a nice person. My knee-jerk response was swift, and the storm I suddenly found myself in seemed to swallow up any bit of my sanity.

It was a seven-week bathroom renovation that also included renovating part of our bedroom and my husband's office. What should have been a standard three- or four-week job turned into a seven-week nightmare. I joked with Greg that our wedding vows were being put into practice and that the "for better or for worse" was tilting into the "for worse" area. I was being stretched, and I was certain I would have the stretch marks to prove it!

How many of us get sucked into watching all those home renovation and improvement shows on television? It's hard to resist the continual barrage of channel after channel wrapping up their pretty-packaged segment in just an hour. One flippin' hour of these gorgeous women slinging a sledgehammer without a trace of sweat or one hair on their heads out of place—I mean, c'mon, let's be real: I wasn't even helping my husband with this ridiculous renovation and I looked like I had aged several years!

The first inconvenience reared its ugly head soon after my husband thought he'd surprise me by turning our seven-foot ceiling into a lovely-sounding nine-foot ceiling. What's not to love about taller ceilings in a fairly cramped en-suite bathroom? I'll give you a word: BATS!

One night, as Greg was standing outside, looking up at the area close to where he'd begin pushing through the ceiling the following day, he heard a funny sound. He was certain he was hearing the scurrying of rats up in the soffit and was more than just a little annoyed. He stood there, wondering how he would tackle the project of eliminating the rodents, when suddenly, bat after bat flew out from underneath the roof into the evening sky on their quest to digest the plethora of summer bugs filling the night air. Things had just shifted from bad to worse and Greg wasn't hanging around to count the convoy of the little fanged vampires making a beeline for their next meal.

Bats in our attic—the same attic to which he was about to expose our bathroom the very next day! Greg placed a call to the local bat specialist and was informed that bats are a protected species and can't be exterminated. We were told we could do absolutely nothing until the autumn when they (and their babies) evacuated the premises. This specialist told my husband to poke his head into our attic and count how many were up there. He said if there were only a hundred, it wasn't a big deal, but if there were thousands, then we had a problem (no kidding!).

So, with much trepidation, Greg took his flashlight and scouted out the attic the next day. To our utmost relief, the winged creatures were only in the soffit and had not set up residence in our attic. Whatever was there had flown out. Catastrophe diverted! But that was just the beginning of countless weird and unpredictable problems arising. Through it all, my husband stayed the course and worked tirelessly on what I told him would be our last home project. It turned out to be a beautiful renovation, up until the night when I obviously needed some more character building.

It happened the night I was cooking dinner and heard a strange noise coming from our laundry room. Uh-oh. I was too busy in the kitchen to try to figure out what was happening, so I asked Greg to check out the unusual sound. After not hearing any response from him, I stepped into our laundry room to find my husband leaned over our hot water tank with his head hanging down in a somewhat defeated look.

Oh great. Now what?

Drip, drip, drip.

I looked up at the ceiling to see full pockets of water dripping in a fairly steady stream from our ugly popcorn ceiling (and I had already vowed to never go through another renovation, so that ugly ceiling is staying put). Right above the ceiling was Greg's masterpiece, the shower he had just spent hours tiling, grouting, and fighting with.

At that point, my anxiety overwhelmed me as sanity took the nearest exit. I envisioned the entire shower needing to be ripped apart to get to the plumbing, or, worse, our entire upstairs bathroom crashing through our laundry room ceiling. Our nearly redone home would once again be in upheaval and the chaos I had just endured for seven weeks would now have a new number assigned to it. Eight? Nine? Ten?

ANXIETY CAN BE RELENTLESS; IT TRIES DESPERATELY TO FIND A LANDING PAD ON A HEART THAT FORGETS TO TRUST.

I told my husband, angrily, to contact our insurance company immediately because I wasn't leaving this latest surprise in the hands of an amateur. I was *mad*! I felt completely out of control and it wasn't pretty.

During my temper tantrum downstairs, Greg was upstairs on the phone. He was avoiding my boisterous outburst as he waited in the queue with other callers probably dealing with similar house renovation nightmares. He patiently listened to the elevator music playing in his ear, with a woman's voice interjecting every few minutes, thanking him for waiting and telling him to stay on the line; his call would be answered by the next available agent.

During my twenty-minute tirade, God arrested me in the middle of my rant and I sheepishly responded to His *thwack* and walked upstairs to find Greg. I knew I needed to immediately apologize to him and ask God to forgive me.

I asked Greg to hang up the phone and he looked at me like I honestly had gone mad. I repeated that he needed to hang up, which meant he'd lose his place in the queue to place an insurance claim. He begrudgingly hung up and looked at me, annoyed. "Now what?"

Stepping out of anger, anxiety, and frustration, I chose to step into humility, admit my failure, and apologize. Yes, it's a choice. Twenty minutes was far too long to let my emotions take the driver's seat! How many of us struggle with letting our emotions dictate a situation? I was at a crossroads, at which point the crisis could've spun even further out of control. I chose to heed wisdom and apologize—apologize for lashing out in anger, for spinning out of control, and for not taking it to God first.

I grabbed Greg's hands and asked him to forgive me and then asked God to forgive me. My pent-up tears turned into a geyser as I immediately felt peace swaddle me like a much-needed heavenly blanket.

I then asked God to give us a strategy for the problem. At that exact moment, God downloaded a complete video into Greg's mind, showing him what the problem was and even how it happened. He gave him a step-by-step solution. Greg later explained it was like a YouTube tutorial video guide.

When I had finished my desperate prayer for help, Greg gave me a huge hug as a mischievous smile crossed his face as he told me it was going to be okay. Hallelujah—that's what I needed to hear. He explained that God had just given him the answer in the craziest way and that it would be an easy fix; nothing would need to be ripped apart. How thankful we both were for this answer to prayer in a desperate situation.

As we both reflected on what had happened, we were amazed at God's faithfulness, even when I was coming unglued. It was like He was waiting for me to snap out of it and practise what I preach. I'm certain He had something to do with the agent not responding immediately to our emergency call. Those twenty minutes it took for me to calm down gave me time to intercept what could've cost us a lot of money had an agent actually responded and sent someone to our home. Instead, the total cost of the fix was a whopping five cents.

It's important we heed the "nudges of heaven" and turn to God first in any situation. Life is going to throw us curveballs—that's just a given. It's how we respond that matters. Are we going to have knee-jerk reactions that will serve only to spiral us out of control? Or are we going to take a step back and take the situation to the Father Who is waiting for us to come to Him?

In hindsight, our home would've been much more peaceful had I not responded in anger. God would've still given Greg the play-by-play video of how to fix the problem and no people would've been hurt in the making of this story. We will always have a choice to make.

I'm reminded of a similar situation that had taken place earlier in the same year.

It was a beautiful sunny, spring day. A perfect day to play eighteen holes of golf with my family. I had anticipated this game for several weeks and was looking forward to having my father join Greg, Brooke, and me on the golf course. It would be a wonderful time for making memories… or so I thought.

I awoke that morning, completely exhausted from having hot flashes every hour throughout the night. The double dose of caffeine for breakfast hadn't even made a dent on my sagging eyelids. The one-and-a-half-hour drive to meet up with my dad at the course had me agitated right out of the driveway. By the time we arrived at the scenic golf course, my attitude was in desperate need of an adjustment.

As we walked over to the range, I noticed more people than usual waiting for the next available space to warm up and practise their swing. We figured out later that the golf course was having a big promotion on various clubs. Members were at the range, test-driving the new brands before teeing off. Needless to say, it was a tad busy, and I soon dismissed the thought of any chance of having a leisurely game. My intuition proved accurate on our very first hole.

Shortly after the four of us teed off, I noticed a smaller team right behind us eagerly waiting. I was hoping they would give us a little slack with our less-than-straight shots that veered off the fairway. Nope. They must've had hot flashes throughout the night as well, because they were less than patient with us. By the second hole, they were up in our grill, launching balls at us as we were still on the green. The next few holes only got worse and I became extremely agitated. At that point, I was only playing "best ball," trying to accommodate their obnoxious behaviour. My family seemed content taking their time and were able to ignore the group on our tail; however, I completely unravelled. I was unsuccessful in trying to get my family to speed things up. I felt anxiety tighten its grip on me and I snapped. I honestly just wanted to go home; this wasn't what I had signed up for.

I realized I was about to ruin the entire day for everyone, so with a "nudge from heaven," I stepped away from my family and went to the opposite side of my golf cart. I took my phone out of my pocket, turned the ringer off, and set it in the drink holder of the cart. I placed one hand up on the roof and decided I needed to have a talk with God.

Hidden away from my family, I had a private conversation with God, "Hey, God, I'm not doing well! I need your help. I *really* need your help."

Brooke came around the cart to check on me; as she did, she noticed my phone.

"Mom!" she exclaimed. "You're dialing 911!"

"What are you talking about?" I asked, confused.

She quickly picked up my phone, pressed a button, then placed my phone back in the drink holder. A moment later, I noticed a number coming through on the display of my silenced phone.

"Hello?" I answered.

"Hello," a professional woman's voice responded. "I see that someone just called 911 from this number. Do you need our help?"

I nervously began to laugh and apologized profusely. I tried explaining to her that I must've pressed something when I placed my phone in the tight space of the drink holder of the golf cart.

"Is someone prompting you to say this?" the woman asked, as if to ensure I was telling the truth.

A little thrown off, I replied, "Umm, no, I'm legit at the golf course, playing really crappy. So, yes, I need help—with my golf game!"

I heard laughter on the other end of the phone. "Okay, well, have a good day and a really good rest of your golf game. I hope it gets better for you!"

We both hung up. I began to laugh at the situation and immediately thanked God for answering my cry for help. That conversation with the dispatcher diffused my anger and got me out of my "funk."

When we ask God for help, He answers. Sometimes it's a little unconventional, but he always answers our S.O.S.

> *I cried out to the Lord in the middle of my troubles; I cried out to my God. He listened to my voice from his sanctuary, and my call for help was heard.* (2 Samuel 22:7, ISV)

EPILOGUE

The common denominator throughout my life has been the "nudge of heaven" (with the occasional *thwack!*), with each experience woven into every story on my journey. I've never journeyed alone, however; the Lord has been beside me with each step I've taken.

There have been stories in which my footprints have aligned close to the Lord's steps. On other occasions, He has scooped me up in His arms as my little feet teetered precariously close to the edge of a cliff.

The rescuing power of God is evident in my marriage, as my husband, Greg, and I are edging closer to celebrating our 30th wedding anniversary. I am extremely thankful the Lord carried me to safety when I was oblivious to the strategy of the enemy wanting to destroy my marriage and family.

As a mother, I have reflected on the incredible journey of parenting. What a privilege it has been to raise three wonderful children. I have been in awe, watching them have their own experiences with "nudges from heaven." My nest is now empty, but the space is filled with incredible memories of the goodness of God. My adult children are now making their own decisions as they respond to the Lord's voice and follow God's call on their lives. Youth With A Mission (YWAM) continues to be a thread woven into the fabric of our family's DNA.

My prayer is that each of you would know how much God loves you and you would experience such a close relationship with Jesus as you journey through life.

You have been marked with purpose and destiny and each decision you make, leading you closer to, or further away from, some awe-inspiring encounters.

While we still have breath in our lungs and ink in our pen, let's purpose to live each day, anticipating the next adventure God has up His sleeve for us. And He has big sleeves!

ABOUT THE AUTHOR

Tammy Roy is a first-time Canadian author with a passion for life, faith, and family. She is a gym manager who lives on Vancouver Island in beautiful British Columbia. This fun-loving West Coast mamma and her husband Greg are recent empty-nesters.

Their oldest, Tyler, has lived in Perth, Australia for the past eight years. Recently married in a summer pandemic wedding, he and his beautiful British bride Rachel are part of a YWAM team, pioneering a base in Broome, Australia.

Jordan works in the construction sector in Victoria, British Columbia. He is Red-Seal-certified in sprinkler fitting and fire suppression.

Brooke lives in the Kimberley Region of Western Australia, along with her brother and sister-in-law. She is part of the pioneering YWAM team in Broome.

Tammy and Greg have a passion for seeing people's lives healed and transformed by the power of God. They are part of the leadership team at Christian Fellowship Centre in Qualicum Beach.

CONTACT:
nudgesfromheaven@yahoo.com
www.facebook.com/TammyRoyCreations
www.instagram.com/nudgesfromheaven